THE
HOLY
ROMAN
EMPIRE

BARBARA STOLLBERG-RILINGER

Translated and with a Preface by Yair Mintzker

THE HOLY ROMAN EMPIRE

A SHORT HISTORY

PRINCETON UNIVERSITY PRESS

PRINCETON AND OXFORD

First published in Germany as *Das Heilige Römische Reich Deutscher Nation: Vom Ende des Mittelalters bis 1806* by Barbara Stollberg-Rilinger.

© Verlag C. H. Beck oHG, Munich 2013

Copyright © 2018 by Princeton University Press

Requests for permission to reproduce material from this work should be sent to permissions@press.princeton.edu

Published by Princeton University Press

41 William Street, Princeton, New Jersey 08540

6 Oxford Street, Woodstock, Oxfordshire OX20 1TR

press.princeton.edu

All Rights Reserved

LCCN 2018931868

ISBN 978-0-691-17911-7

British Library Cataloging-in-Publication Data is available

Editorial: Brigitta van Rheinberg and Amanda Peery

Production Editorial: Sara Lerner

Text and Jacket Design: Lorraine Doneker

Jacket Credit: Jacket image courtesy of Shutterstock

Production: Jacquie Poirier

Publicity: Jodi Price

Copyeditor: Cynthia Buck

The translation of this work was funded by Geisteswissenschaften International— Translation Funding for Humanities and Social Sciences from Germany, a joint initiative of the Fritz Thyssen Foundation, the German Federal Foreign Office, the collecting society VG WORT and the Börsenverein des Deutschen Buchhandels (German Publishers & Booksellers Association).

This book has been composed in Minion Pro

Printed on acid-free paper. ∞

Printed in the United States of America

1 3 5 7 9 10 8 6 4 2

CONTENTS

TRANSLATOR'S PREFACE TO THE ENGLISH EDITION

The little book you are holding in your hands is no ordinary work, and the scholar who wrote it is not your run-of-the-mill historian. In a little over a hundred pages, Barbara Stollberg-Rilinger achieves the seemingly impossible: a concise, elegant, and utterly enlightening account of the immensely complex and often outright chaotic Holy Roman Empire in the early modern period (1495–1806). It is a book that wears its theoretical sophistication lightly and its learning gracefully. And although it contains a powerful and clear story line, it is also a deep, multilayered work. I myself have read it many times since its original publication in German in 2007, and I have never failed to draw inspiration from it or to discover new and exciting insights in its pages.

Understanding the exact reasons for this book's many accomplishments is not a requirement for learning a great deal from it. Indeed, readers who know nothing at all about the Holy Roman Empire of the German Nation may skip this short introduction and return to it only once they have finished reading the book in its entirety. Nevertheless, more seasoned students of early modern Europe may definitely benefit from a few introductory remarks about Barbara Stollberg-Rilinger's career and theoretical approach. Stollberg-Rilinger's book is unique not only in what it tells us about the Holy Roman Empire. It is also special in how it does it.

Stollberg-Rilinger is the foremost living historian of the Holy Roman Empire of the German Nation in the early modern period. She was educated at the University of Cologne, where she studied under the supervision of Johannes Kunisch—an important scholar in his own right, who was one of the earliest German historians to write about the early modern period as such. Kunisch was an expert on a long list of classic themes in German historiography, including absolutism, military history, and state-building processes (*Staatlichkeit*). Throughout her career, Stollberg-Rilinger addressed similarly "big" topics to those of her *Doktorvater*. She did so, however, with an important twist.

Already during her time at Cologne, Stollberg-Rilinger began to draw inspiration from a new wave of scholarship done primarily at the University of Bielefeld by such scholars as Reinhard Koselleck in history and especially Niklas Luhmann in sociology. The cross-pollination between Cologne and Bielefeld proved decisive for the rest of her career. It created a unique blend of classical historiographical themes, on the one hand, and cutting-edge theoretical approaches in cultural studies, sociology, and anthropology, on the other hand. Early products of this approach included Stollberg-Rilinger's fabulous dissertation on the metaphorical language of European absolutism ("Der Staat als Maschine: Zur politischen Metaphorik des absoluten Fürstenstaats," 1986) and a habilitation thesis on the representation strategies of territorial estates in the late phase of the Holy Roman Empire ("Vormünder des Volkes? Konzepte landständischer Repräsentation in der Spätphase des Alten Reichs," 1994).

The real breakthrough came in 1997. That year, Stollberg-Rilinger was appointed professor of early modern history at the University of Münster. There, together with the medievalist Gerd Althoff and other colleagues, she began a long-term project on symbolic communication in the early modern period that in the next twenty years would lead to dozens of important publications. An early essay on the topic of symbolic communication set the theoretical terms for much that would follow ("Zeremoniell als politisches Verfahren: Rangordnung und Rangstreit als Sturkturmerkmale des frühneuzeitlichen Reichstags," 1997). In 2013, the essay would be expanded into a book that was recently also translated into English as *The Emperor's Old Clothes: Constitutional History and the Symbolic Language of the Holy Roman Empire* (Berghahn Books, 2015). After completing the present book, readers interested in learning more about Stollberg-Rilinger's approach to the history of the Empire may turn to *The Emperor's Old Clothes* as well as to Stollberg-Rilinger's latest book: a prize-winning biography of Austrian empress Maria Theresa (German edition 2017; English translation forthcoming from Princeton University Press in 2018).

Inspired in the first place by the sociological approach of Peter Berger and Thomas Luckmann, and then by a long list of works by other scholars, including Niklas Luhmann, Max Weber, Norbert Elias, Erving Goffman, Clifford Geertz, and Pierre Bourdieu, Stollberg-Rilinger's main theoretical claim is that the constitutional history of premodern polities cannot be separated from their procedures and ceremonies. These are not mere sideshows or dim reflections of what "really matters"—for example, royal decisions, written constitutional and legal documents, or grand political ideas. Rather, procedures and ceremonies are themselves extraordinarily important political realms. Unlike earlier German constitutional historians who emphasized written documents, Stollberg-Rilinger focuses on the symbolic language of the king's court, the Imperial diet, and the city council. In this, she relies on and develops further Luhmann's sociological theory, especially his early work *Legitimation durch Verfahren* (1969). In her view, who sat next to whom at the Imperial diet, who arrived when to a new emperor's court, who wore what for which enfeoffment ceremony, or who had the right to speak first at a territorial diet were fundamental political issues in premodern social systems, even or especially when such systems produced few, if

any, written documents. That contemporaries argued about such issues much more than about the creation of written documents is no
coincidence. They did so for a reason.

Lest all of this sound too abstract, consider for a moment the
somewhat antiquated way in which Americans elect their president
today. As recent events have demonstrated all too clearly, both the
composition of the electoral college and the resistance to changing
anything about it have had decisive influence on the fate of the country. That almost all Americans accept as legitimate the election of
Donald J. Trump as president of the United States is very much a
product of a series of fictions such as the idea that the outcome of
the elections represents the will of the American people even though
not all citizens cast their votes and the popular vote was not identical
to the electoral one. Thus, procedure, decision-making, and political
legitimacy are quite inseparable in this case. Or think about the fact
that American juries deliberate behind closed doors and not in public, that they do so orally and not in writing, and that they are in-
structed to refrain from discussing the case with any nonjurors or,
until the deliberations begin, even with their peers. These are not
trivial matters: in the criminal justice system, procedures often decide matters of life and death. What we decide often depends on how
we decide.

Stollberg-Rilinger is too good a storyteller to spell out many of
these issues in the present book, which targets a broad audience.
Like any master builder, once her work is standing, she dismantles
the scaffolding and lets the building carry its own weight. Nevertheless, attentive readers will find dozens of examples in this book
where Stollberg-Rilinger's analysis follows the same procedural logic
outlined here: in her historical accounts of institutions like the Imperial diet or the two supreme Imperial courts; in her descriptions of
events ranging from the negotiations leading to the Peace of Westphalia (1648) to the entire evolution of the Protestant Reformation;

and in her discussions of long-term structural processes such as the transition from the late Middle Ages to the early modern period around the year 1500.

Related to her emphasis on the importance of procedures is Stollberg-Rilinger's insistence that the Holy Roman Empire existed at a time when religion, politics, and the economy were not yet separate spheres. The Empire consequently followed a quintessentially premodern logic. To describe it as a proto nation-state (as the German historian Georg Schmidt, for instance, did in a controversial book he published in 1999) is to miss both what was unique about it and what distinguishes it from modern states. Unlike some of Schmidt's followers, Stollberg-Rilinger also uses terms like "progress" and "national unity" very sparingly. Her Holy Roman Empire is not a homogeneous polity with its own "intentions." As a premodern, composite, complex polity, it always looked different from different angles and affected its members in very uneven ways. The Empire was above all a political space of conflicting interests, motives, and effects. Only as such does its history begin to make sense.

Historians must navigate carefully between the Scylla of overwhelming their readers with too much information and the Charybdis of overly abstract theories. As a wise historian once said, history without theory is like a boat without a sail—it wanders aimlessly—while theory without historical facts is like a sail without a boat—it goes nowhere. In her mastery of the sociological literature and her erudition, and with her elegant writing style, Stollberg-Rilinger strikes exactly the right balance. It is my hope that the present translation will help readers understand better the history of the Holy Roman Empire between 1495 and 1806 while also giving them a first glimpse into Stollberg-Rilinger's pathbreaking historical approach.

—Yair Mintzker
Princeton, New Jersey, September 2017

A NOTE ON THE TRANSLATION

This translation follows the usage rules established by Thomas A. Brady Jr. in his *German Histories in the Age of Reformations* (Cambridge University Press, 2009, xv). Whenever possible, I tried to use English equivalents to both place names and persons ("Cologne" not "Köln," "Charles V" not "Karl V"). I capitalized the terms "Empire" and "Imperial" only when they refer to the historic polity of the Holy Roman Empire, and "Church" is capitalized when the entire Western Church is meant. When the English-speaking literature was inconsistent in its translation of an important term, I often kept the German original (for example, *Reichsregiment*) so as to allow, I hope, for easier navigation in the text.

The Holy Roman Empire in the early modern period. *Source*: Angelika Solibieda, cartomedia, Karlsruhe.

THE HOLY ROMAN EMPIRE

INTRODUCTION

Shortly after American troops entered Nuremberg on April 20, 1945, they seized the medieval crown of the Holy Roman Emperor, which had been transferred to Nuremberg from Vienna seven years earlier at the personal order of Adolf Hitler. The rapidly approaching victory of the Allies over Nazi Germany could hardly have found a more powerful symbolic expression. What the soldiers seized that day was an object that symbolized perfectly the tortuous course of German history. For twelve years, the Nazis had appropriated the history of the Holy Roman Empire of the German Nation for their own purposes, using it to propagate the myth of Germany's supposed "historical mission" to expand beyond its existing political boundaries and reach world domination. Hitler's "Thousand Year Empire," however, lasted only twelve years—a stark contrast to the first empire whose name it invoked. When American GIs played with the medieval crown, jestingly putting it on their heads, they couldn't have made that fact any clearer.

The consequences of the Nazi appropriation of the history of the Holy Roman Empire are present even today. *Reich*, the German word for "empire," immediately invokes the Third Reich—the Nazi dictatorship of 1933 to 1945. The Third Reich overshadows the two other German empires that came before it: the Second Empire, or Imperial Germany (Kaiserreich), founded by Otto von Bismarck under Prussian hegemony in 1871 and lasting until 1918; and especially the first

Figure 1. The crown of the Holy Roman Emperor. *Source*: National Archives, Washington, DC.

Figure 2. Private First Class Ivan Babcock tries on the crown of the Holy Roman Emperor. The gold and pearl crown was stored with other treasures in a cave captured by US First Army troops in Germany in April 1945. *Source*: US Army, photo 111-SC-205728.

empire, the medieval and early modern Holy Roman Empire, which lasted (depending on one's point of view) anywhere between eight hundred and close to a thousand years. This first empire has hardly left any imprint at all on the collective memory of Germans (let alone other Europeans), although it undoubtedly shaped important aspects of modern German political history. If we want to understand what this first or "Old Empire" was, we consequently must begin with the history of its reception in the nineteenth and twentieth centuries. This history has shaped the Holy Roman Empire's modern image to such an extent that any attempt to simply ignore it is doomed to fail.

The Holy Roman Empire of the German Nation had a clear ending. On August 6, 1806, Emperor Francis II abdicated the Imperial throne under pressure from Napoleon and solemnly dissolved "the bond, which has hitherto tied Us to the body politic of the German Empire." Five days earlier, on August 1, sixteen Imperial members had declared their secession from the Empire, basing their decision on the fact that "the ties, which in the past had united the different members of the German body politic to one another, have in fact already been dissolved." Thus, at the very same time that national unity became a central political goal across Europe, German political unity ceased to exist. In the following decades, with the Holy Roman Empire no longer a political reality, it increasingly became an object for historical research, political mythology, and sometimes a combination of both.

During the nineteenth century, the recently dissolved Empire did not become a common reference point for the nationalistic-romantic aspirations for German unity. Far from it. Nineteenth-century Germans viewed the early modern Empire as a ramshackle, ridiculous, and even monstrous polity. It was rather the history of the medieval Empire, beginning with the pope's coronation of the Saxon prince Otto I as "German king" in 962, that appealed to nineteenth-century German nationalists. The latter claimed to have found in the distant past, during the early and High Middle Ages, a glorious empire under whose aegis German kings ruled as emperors with supposedly supreme power over all of Western Christianity. Everything that happened after the time of the great kings and emperors of the Saxon, Salian, and Hohenstaufen dynasties seemed, on the other hand, to resemble a decline-and-fall story of the medieval Imperial power and German political unity. The erstwhile powerful universal Empire continuously fragmented into its constituting parts—the princely territories—as individual German princes expanded their powers at the expense of the emperor by usurping his prerogatives one by one.

The common nineteenth-century depiction of a great and powerful medieval German state was a backward projection of modern nationalistic wishful thinking, an anachronistic image that had little to do with historical reality. The power and authority so often ascribed to medieval emperors by nineteenth-century historians had never in fact really been theirs. In the Middle Ages, political power and authority were generated through the interaction of three institutions—kingship, aristocracy, and the Church—and in this interaction the king played primarily the role of moderator. The medieval Empire was never a state in the modern sense of the term. If it ever developed any kind of formal institutions (which is debatable), these appeared only after the year 1500, during the transition from the Middle Ages to what historians now call the early modern period. For proponents of the idea of a great medieval empire, however, the Holy Roman Empire's decline was already under way by 1500, a process that gained further momentum after the Peace of Westphalia ended the Thirty Years' War in 1648. According to this line of thinking, after Westphalia the Empire fell under the auspices of the "French archenemy," became merely "a pawn in Great Powers politics," and disintegrated into a multitude of small states—a supposedly linear development that led to the inevitable dissolution of the Holy Roman Empire during the Napoleonic Wars.

Finally, it was not the Empire in its entirety but rather its two most prominent former members—Austria and Prussia—that formed the nuclei of powerful modern states in the nineteenth century: Austria-Hungary, on the one hand, and Imperial Germany (the Second Empire), on the other hand. This fact split the German national movement into two camps. The first camp strove to reestablish the Old Empire as a predominantly Catholic polity, including Austria. This political solution was known as "large Germany." The other camp sought to create a principally Protestant nation-state, led by Prussia and excluding Austria. Its political solution was consequently known as "small Germany." Both camps failed to reach their goals during the decades following the dissolution of the Holy Roman Empire. Only with Bismarck's establishment of the Second Empire in 1871 did the "small German" solution become reality, and this Bismarckian empire had admittedly very little to do with the Holy Roman Empire.

Nineteenth-century German historians, who reached the peak of their influence and prestige in the middle decades of the century, viewed themselves as the practitioners of a specifically national scholarly endeavor. Two different states—the Prussian-dominated Kaiserreich, on the one hand, and Austria-Hungary, on the other hand—claimed to be the true heirs of the Old Empire, and both employed historians to provide them with the necessary political genealogy to bolster their authority and legitimacy. Integrating the old Imperial history into Austria's new national history proved a relatively easy task. From 1452 until the dissolution of the Empire in 1806, almost all Holy Roman Emperors had belonged to the Habsburg dynasty. The last Holy Roman Emperor, Francis II, crowned himself Austrian emperor in 1804, and during the nineteenth century the Habsburg monarchy continued to be a transnational polity, just as the Old Empire had been throughout its existence. The situation was quite different in the Kaiserreich to the north, where, in contrast to Austria-Hungary, historians faced the much trickier task of constructing a historical narrative that would connect the medieval Empire, the rise of Prussia in the early modern period, and the creation of a predominantly Protestant, Prussian-led Kaiserreich in 1871. Proponents of the "small German" solution began their story with the decline of the late medieval Empire. Out of the debris of this empire, new national energies emerged in the form of Martin Luther's Reformation and the actions of Germany's Protestant princes, chief among them the electors of Brandenburg (later to become the kings of Prussia). According to nineteenth-century German historians, these Brandenburg-Prussian rulers were the ones who took over the national mission from the declining Empire and turned Prussia into the nucleus around which a new German nation-state could finally crystallize.

Whether in the Austrian or the Prussian-German historiographical traditions, the story of the early modern Holy Roman Empire and its institutions went largely by the wayside. Historians of both traditions wrote primarily from the perspective of their ruling dynasties—the Habsburgs in Austria, the Hohenzollerns in the Kaiserreich. Only in 1938, after Hitler supposedly "brought Austria back home" by annexing it to his Third Reich, did the two separate story lines seem to finally converge. Hitler's decision to transfer the Imperial crown from Vienna to Nuremberg that same year symbolized this historical convergence by way of the two national story lines' supposed origins in a common medieval past. German and Austrian historians were all too eager to help Hitler in sustaining this historical myth, and their efforts continued to influence the popular historical imagination (at least in West Germany) even after the collapse of the Third Reich in 1945. Indeed, in many ways this account continues to influence the German historical imagination to the present day. To give just one example: in textbooks about their national history, German schoolchildren still read much more about the rise of early modern Prussia than about the institutions of the Holy Roman Empire during the same period.

Only in the 1960s did historians begin to look at the Old Empire with fresh eyes. It was a time of a major generational shift in German academe, and a younger generation of historians finally began to break away from the value system of the old nationalistic historiography. Further contributing to the reevaluation of the Holy Roman Empire was the fact that the territory of West Germany, founded in 1949, encompassed the same regions in western and southwestern Germany where the structures of the Old Empire had once exerted their greatest influence. A western and southwestern Catholic perspective slowly pushed aside the old Protestant-Prussian point of view of previous generations of historians. A final push for the reevaluation of the early modern Empire came when German universities started institutionalizing the field of early modern history (the period between 1500 and 1800). Following the emergence of this field, historians began to investigate the constitutional history of the early modern Empire, researching the political, legal, and social structures characteristic of its core lands in contradistinction to the nation-building processes that took place in Austria and Prussia around the same time. The pendulum now swung starkly the other way. What previous historians had considered the Empire's main weaknesses now seemed to be its primary strengths. The structural deficits of the Holy Roman Empire—especially its lack of a common military defense—appeared to be, in the postwar context, its virtues. Before the German reunification of 1991, and even more so thereafter, the early modern Empire offered historians a new, morally neutral object for national identification: a large, peaceful, defense-oriented, and federative community in the middle of Europe that Germany's neighbors had had no reason to fear in the past and of which modern Germans could be proud in the present with a good conscience and without raising alarm.

By the second half of the twentieth century, the Old Empire also began to appear in discussions about European integration. At least at first glance, there are indeed some interesting parallels between the Old Empire and the European Union, including the large autonomy enjoyed by the two polities' respective individual members, the weakness of their central institutions, and the constant need for consensus in the political processes characteristic of both. Such seeming parallels led some German historians and politicians to view the early modern Holy Roman Empire as a positive model for a new Europe, a kind of ready-made predecessor for a European Union that lacked common historical symbols or legitimizing traditions. After all, just like the Holy Roman Empire, the European Union too is a supra-regional, non-expansionist, peaceful legal framework. Of course, not all European politicians showed enthusiasm for such a comparison between a quintessentially *German* empire and a distinctly *European* union.

The historical reception of the Holy Roman Empire in the nineteenth and twentieth centuries, which I have sketched here with only very broad brushstrokes, had one final and very important consequence. The fact that the Empire was not a homogeneous polity and that it contained many internal contradictions has lent its history to different interpretations and various deployments by a wide spectrum of political actors. This fact often obstructs our path to a proper understanding of the Empire's history. In writing the following pages, I have attempted to refrain from using the Empire's history in order to make a political statement about the present. Instead, I have chosen to highlight the Empire's specific premodern and alien nature, its ambiguities, and its many overlapping layers. I have attempted, in other words, to historicize it. I am very much aware that even such an attempt can be interpreted as a political move. Highlighting the strange and alien character of the Empire (or of any other object of historical study, for that matter) could be ascribed to a supposedly "postmodern" stance that emphasizes values such as cultural diversity, a sensitivity to the kaleidoscopic nature of all historical realities, and a deep suspicion of any attempt to reach one single, unquestionable truth. I believe nonetheless that it is exactly this kind of approach that allows us to be even-handed when investigating the past. Only thus can we concentrate not on what the past means in the present, but on what the past was when it was not yet the past.

1

WHAT WAS THE HOLY ROMAN EMPIRE OF THE GERMAN NATION?

The very name "Holy Roman Empire of the German Nation" hints at this polity's ambiguous, perhaps even peculiar, character. It was "Roman" but also "German"; it was an empire, but it also belonged to a specific "nation"; and somehow it was supposed to be "holy." What was it, then?

As a polity, the Empire largely escapes modern constitutional categories, and so it is far easier to say what it wasn't than to determine what it actually was. The Holy Roman Empire was neither a state nor a confederation of states. It had no systematic written constitution, it acknowledged no equality before the law—not even as an ideal— and it did not impart Imperial citizenship on its inhabitants. The Empire furthermore did not encompass a territory with clearly defined boundaries, and it possessed no sovereign, supreme authority, no central executive, no bureaucracy, and no standing army. In short, the Holy Roman Empire lacked almost all those characteristics that define modern states as such. Using modern constitutional categories to define it might consequently lead to a negative evaluation of its history almost by default. To understand what the Empire actually was, we must describe it on its own terms and refrain from using modern concepts that, throughout its long history, had always remained foreign to it.

While it existed, the Empire was most commonly imagined as a loose political body. It contained very different members, or "limbs," that formed individual ties to a common overlord, or "head" (the emperor), through oaths of personal fealty. Generally speaking, the cohesiveness of this body politic declined over the course of the Middle Ages, but around the year 1500 the Empire evolved along new lines and took more solid institutional forms. Despite rising political tensions and even outright open conflicts, the Empire lasted for another three hundred years. It ceased to exist only under the impact of the French Revolution and the Napoleonic Wars.

In contrast to the relative independence of the political realm in modern systems of government, the political system of the Holy Roman Empire was still tightly connected to the social and religious structures of its day. Its constitution resembled less a systematic modern legal code and much more a colorful fabric woven out of both new and old threads. These threads included symbolic and ceremonial practices, formal and informal rules, some occasionally negotiated consensual decisions and contracts, a few fixed, written fundamental laws (*leges fundamentales*), many traditional forms of legitimacy, and a multitude of incompatible and indeed conflicting legal-political claims. Within this complex system, every rule had its exceptions and every abstract definition was restricted in practice. Moreover, different Imperial members perceived the Empire's basic structure differently, depending on their particular point of view, and these perceptions constantly changed and evolved over time. All of this makes it close to impossible to muster a clear-cut definition of the Empire. If I nevertheless attempt to do so here, the reader should take it with a grain of salt. In reality, things were always much more complicated.

A good starting point for our discussion is the Empire's very title. The complete name "The Holy Roman Empire of the German Nation" appeared for the first time only at the end of the fifteenth century, and it would never be the sole—let alone the official—title of the Empire. According to an often-quoted quip by the eighteenth-century French philosopher Voltaire, the Holy Roman Empire was neither holy nor Roman, nor indeed an empire at all. This witticism aside, a close investigation of the individual elements in the Empire's title does reveal important clues about its composite—part medieval, part early modern—character.

Here, first of all, is the term "empire," *imperium* in Latin, which denotes a supreme overlordship, namely that of the emperor. During the Middle Ages, "imperium" was a common synonym for the office of the emperor himself. Its primary meaning was not a specific territory in which the emperor ruled supreme, but a universal, transpersonal authority that was not bound to a specific region or people.

The term "Roman" placed the Empire within the ancient European imperial tradition. As the first medieval ruler of the West, Charlemagne had himself crowned emperor by the pope in the year 800, thus transforming himself from a king of one Germanic tribe (the Franks) into a ruler with universal aspirations and a sacred aura. Charlemagne's empire disintegrated not long after his death. But Otto the Great, Charlemagne's distant descendant, revived the same idea in 962 when he related his east Frankish (later German) kingship to the imperial traditions of ancient Rome. From that point on, almost all German kings also possessed the title of "Roman emperor." The idea of *translatio imperii*—the uninterrupted passing, or "translation," of rulership from the ancient Romans to the Franks and then further down to the great medieval German dynasties— was obviously a fiction. At the same time, it was based on the symbolic act of coronation by the pope, who was the supreme head of the Roman Church. This symbolic act allowed German emperors to claim political authority over all Christians and precedence over all other European rulers. By invoking the idea of *translatio imperii*, medieval emperors placed themselves within the divine history of the ancient Roman empire, the political entity in which Jesus Christ lived and died and which eventually allowed for the spread of the Gospel over the entire known world. Common late antique interpretations of the Book of Daniel also viewed the Roman empire as the last of the four worldly empires, at the fall of which the Antichrist would appear and the Last Judgment take place. These biblical interpretations bolstered the idea of *translatio imperii*. If the world had yet to come to an end, the Roman empire must have continued to exist one way or another.

The ancient Roman empire was not called "holy" (*sacrum* in Latin). Only since the time of Emperor Frederick Barbarossa in the twelfth century does one find this adjective attached to the Empire's title. It was introduced in the context of the hugely contested issue of the supposed subordination of the emperor to the pope, an argument first espoused by Pope Gregory VII in the late eleventh century. By attaching the term "holy" to his title, the emperor's supporters strove to place their lord's authority on equal footing with that of the pope—the temporal sword alongside the ecclesiastical one. They were largely successful in this. Gregory VII's claims for superiority over the emperor were eschewed by his later, less powerful, successors. The term "holy" stuck.

During the early modern period, the connection between the emperor's title and a coronation by the pope was broken once and for all. King Maximilian I started calling himself "elected emperor" in 1508 without having been crowned by the pope. (Indeed, he would not be crowned by the pope for the rest of his life.) Maximilian's grandson and successor, Charles V, was still crowned by the pope (in Bologna in 1530), although he had already been elected king and crowned in the city of Aachen in 1519. Charles's successors, however, consistently claimed the title of emperor on the basis of their election alone. They did so even though the election to "Roman king" and the crowning as "Roman emperor" were really two separate acts—for instance, when the election of a new king took place during the lifetime of an old emperor in order to ensure dynastic continuity. In such a case, the elected Roman king took the Imperial title only upon the death of his predecessor. In general, it was customary for one of the Rhine archbishops (the archbishop of Cologne or, as was the rule in the early modern period, of Mainz) to perform the coronation and unction; after 1562, these ceremonies usually took place in the Imperial city of Frankfurt am Main. The results of the elections were then presented to the pope only as a matter of formality.

Despite the reduced role of the pope in early modern Imperial elections, the "holiness" of the Empire—the claim that it had a sacral or divine character—remained very much alive throughout the period. It even survived the religious schism of the Reformation. The Empire's claim to holiness endured in part because even as late as the eighteenth century almost every form of legitimate European rulership retained a basis in the conception of the "divine right of kings." The insistence on the holiness of the Empire also served as a political way to highlight its supposed supreme position above all other monarchies in the world and bolster the Empire's position vis-à-vis the Ottoman Turks, who threatened southwestern Europe from the late fifteenth century onward. "The Roman Empire is called a Holy Empire," the jurist Johannes Limnaeus could still write in the seventeenth century, "because it is ordained, confirmed, and preserved to this day by the Holy Spirit." Nevertheless, by the eighteenth century Imperial officials increasingly dropped the term "holy" from the Empire's title, using instead the more succinct form "Roman-German Empire" (Imperium Romano-Germanicum) and even, quite simply, "the German Empire."

The last two terms we need to clarify are "German" and "nation." As far as we know, the first time these two words appeared together with "Holy Roman Empire" was in Emperor Frederick III's public peace statute of 1486 (*Landfriedensgesetz*). The term "imperium" itself, when it did not signify the universal, territory-less authority of the emperor, referred to a transnational entity that, according to medieval political philosophy, encompassed three countries: Italy, Gaul (essentially Lorraine and Burgundy in modern-day northeastern France), and Germany. After the late Middle Ages, the German character of the Empire—as opposed to its Latin (i.e., Romance-language-speaking) parts—became more and more pronounced. The emperor had lost his political claims over Italy and Burgundy in the meantime, though he could still theoretically revive them if an opportunity presented itself. But above all, the fact that the most important Imperial institutions—which were established in 1495 and endured until 1806—were relevant only in the Empire's German-speaking parts led to a view of the early modern Empire that concentrated only on its German regions. Further bolstering this view was the fact that important seventeenth-century jurists like Hermann Conring and Samuel Pufendorf employed the new critical historical methods developed by Renaissance humanists to question the validity of the Empire's full title and expose as mere fable the claim that it was a continuation of the ancient Roman empire. In a book on the Imperial constitution he published in 1667 under the pseudonym Severinus de Monzambano, Pufendorf caustically attacked the claim for continuity between the ancient Roman empire and the early modern German one. In his view, such a claim was complete nonsense. All these developments contributed to the increasing emphasis on the German character of the early modern Empire and to the addition of this adjective to its title.

Finally, even though the Imperial title contained the term "nation," one has to be careful not to conflate the meaning of this word with its modern connotations. Early modern Europeans conceived of many different regional groups, such as the Saxons or the Bavarians, as nations (*nationes* in Latin). Alongside the more local or regional identities common in the early modern period, one also finds the early beginnings of a general, supra-regional German identity. The humanists' discovery of *Germania*, a book written by the Roman author Tacitus in the first century CE, contributed to this trend, although Tacitus's depiction of the ancient Germans was quite ambiguous. Next to a common language and shared institutions, it was also the common defense of one's liberties vis-à-vis Emperor Charles V—a man whom German princes deemed a foreigner—that contributed already in the sixteenth century to the rise of a political identification with a larger German "imagined community" or nation.

2

A BODY MADE OF HEAD AND LIMBS

The most common early modern metaphor for the Empire was that of a body with a head and limbs. The head was of course the emperor. He was the one who made it possible for the different limbs to form a coherent body politic in the first place. The common ties to the emperor were the oldest and most important elements in the Imperial constitution. The emperor was the supreme feudal lord, the supreme judge, the supreme preserver of law and peace. And yet he was never an absolute monarch; he was never above the law. In accordance with the consensus-oriented Imperial constitution, the emperor had no right to change arbitrarily anything in the traditional political order and had neither the right nor the power to execute anything to which the other Imperial members objected. He had to rely on the advice and consent of others. This state of affairs, already established during the Middle Ages, became even more pronounced over the course of the early modern period.

In practicing his powers, the emperor was always bound by the consent and participation of the Imperial estates, an understanding enshrined by what later generations would retroactively call the fundamental laws of the Empire (its *leges fundamentales*)— most importantly the Golden Bull (1356), the Religious Peace of Augsburg (1555), the Peace of Westphalia (1648), and the electoral capitulations—which all bore the mark of a contract between the emperor and other Imperial members. Belonging to the emperor alone were the "reservation rights" (*Reservatrechte*): the power to change a person's legal status vis-à-vis society as a whole (for instance, through ennoblement, the legitimization of bastards, or the awarding of academic degrees). Viewed in this light, the Holy Roman Emperor was less a supreme overlord than the top corner of the larger social and political hierarchy, a position that legitimized the whole sociopolitical order and safeguarded its continued existence.

The Imperial members stood vis-à-vis the emperor as a coherent body—the official formula spoke here of "Kaiser und Reich" (emperor *and* Empire). The body's limbs, or members, were an incredibly diverse bunch. They included Imperial electors, princes, counts, prelates, knights, cities, and towns. An important distinction was between members who possessed Imperial immediacy alone and those who also enjoyed the status of an Imperial estate in the strict sense of the term. The former were all those members who recognized only the emperor as their overlord, whereas the latter also possessed "a seat and a vote" (*Sitz und Stimme*) in the most important Imperial institution, the Imperial diet. Well into the sixteenth century, it was not altogether clear—especially in the case of Imperial counts, knights, and cities—who belonged in which group. Imperial members were of extremely diverse character and consisted of both persons and corporations, abbeys and urban communes, ecclesiastical and temporal rulers, powerful polities and relatively weak ones. On one end of the spectrum were the great territorial princes who ruled, essentially uncontested, over huge territorial conglomerates. These princes often played important political roles in European politics as a whole, and some of them were even related through marital ties to the great continental dynasties. Indeed, the Habsburgs, as archdukes of Austria and lords over a long list of other Imperial territories, were Imperial members themselves. On the opposite end of the spectrum stood the Imperial knights who ruled over only a couple of villages and even there possessed only very limited legal authority. It was exactly the extraordinary diversity in Imperial membership that was the hallmark of the Empire's constitutional structure. Different Imperial members influenced, and were influenced by, Imperial politics in highly uneven ways.

The Empire was composed not only of those nobles and corporations who enjoyed Imperial immediacy. Most Imperial estates exercised their rights of lordship over territories in which there were many lower carriers of authority, including noble families, abbeys, religious associations, and urban communes. Such groups too belonged to the Empire, but since they did not enjoy the rights and privileges associated with Imperial immediacy, they were known as territorial, or mediated, estates (*landsässige; mediate Stände*) rather than Imperial ones; their position vis-à-vis their territorial lord was not unlike that of the Imperial estates vis-à-vis the emperor. Just like their Imperial counterparts, the territorial estates were a source of income for their lord, and also like them, they had the right to assemble and represent themselves in (territorial) diets. But whereas in the course of the early modern period the Imperial estates managed to extend their influence on the emperor, the representational rights of territorial estates often shrank. This, however, was not the end of the story. Territorial estates also exercised lordship rights over various dependent persons, including cottagers and peasants, who stood in an even lower, more mediated relationship to the emperor and the Empire than the territorial estates above them. Viewing the Empire from the perspective of the ordinary subject, or the "Common Man" (*der gemeine Mann*)—who exercised authority over his own wife, children, and occasionally also servants and farmhands— reveals many overlapping layers of authority, stretching from the local lord or city council all the way up to the emperor.

The Empire was consequently anything but a homogeneous union of subjects. Modern states impart identical political rights to all their citizens, concentrate sovereignty solely in their own hands, and exercise power exclusively through their own organs. The situation in the Holy Roman Empire could not have been more different. There, different people and groups throughout the sociopolitical hierarchy exercised autonomous political authority while enjoying rights and liberties that were unique to them alone. It goes without saying that under such circumstances the emperor did not exercise a homogeneous political authority over all the myriad Imperial and territorial estates, let alone their respective vassals and subjects. For that exact reason, the Empire also did not possess a clearly demarcated territory, as some modern maps suggest. At the same time, it is important to note that the early modern Empire witnessed a fundamental process of territorialization among its members: political authority evolved from a diverse collection of lordship rights over *persons* to an increasingly homogeneous authority over a particular geographical *space* (including all persons and corporations living or situated within its borders). Territorialization did not develop on the level of the Empire as a whole. Rather, particular Imperial members implemented it in their own lands in their role as territorial lords. Until its dissolution, the Empire itself never became a territorial state, but remained a hierarchical, complex system of ties between persons and corporations, at whose top stood the emperor—the person giving the whole body politic its coherence and legitimacy.

A hallmark of the Imperial constitution was the ability of the great Imperial princes to exercise strong authority within their territories. Their exercise of authority had a decisive impact on the Imperial constitution. In the course of the early modern period, the princes' authority increased until it came close in some cases to what one might roughly call territorial sovereignty. The increase in territorial authority (which, incidentally, had not been perceived as a problem before the fifteenth century) came largely at the emperor's expense and finds its origins already in the Middle Ages. While other European monarchies developed into increasingly centralized systems of government with political power appropriated more or less in the hands of a king and his officials—the French case is especially paradigmatic in this respect—the Holy Roman Empire moved in the opposite direction. There was more than one cause for this. First, ever since the death of Emperor Henry VI in 1197, it had become clear that the Empire was an elective, rather than a hereditary, monarchy. As a consequence, any future king or emperor had to rely on the political support and actual votes of a poorly defined circle of princes known as the Imperial electors (*Kurfürsten*). This reliance fostered mutual dependency and compromise. Second, the medieval Empire never developed a permanent central administration or an executive under the authority of the emperor. (Attempts to do so by the Salian and Hohenstaufen dynasties had failed.) Unlike his French counterpart, for instance, the Holy Roman Emperor did not see his authority strengthened by enfeoffment; vacated fiefdoms did not revert back to him (thus enlarging the territory under his direct control), but were donated immediately to new vassals. The same process also affected the Imperial treasury, which could not profit from the financially very valuable territorial lordship rights or from the rights associated with royal sovereignty like minting, mining, tolls, hunting, and so on. With limited territory and treasure of his own, the emperor lacked sufficient means with which to build an "administrative infrastructure" (Wolfgang Reinhard). For everything he wanted to accomplish in the Empire, whether politically or financially, he had to rely on the support of other Imperial members.

A third factor contributing to the decentralized nature of the medieval Empire was the constant competition with the Church. Ever since its triumph in the investiture controversy of the High Middle Ages, the Catholic Church had largely managed to extricate itself from the tight grip of the emperor. In the following centuries, bishops and abbeys used the political and financial authority bestowed upon them by the Church to strengthen their lordship rights within their individual territories. Thus, next to the Papal States, the Empire became the only European polity in which ecclesiastical dignitaries like archbishops, bishops, abbots, and abbesses could also be temporal rulers and, as such, sometimes Imperial members as well.

Last but not least was the issue of the Empire's sheer size. Communicating across its many provinces was not an easy task under the typical conditions of the Middle Ages and the early modern period. Until well into the sixteenth century, there was no postal system in central Europe, and crossing the Empire from one end to the other could take an individual as long as thirty days. The vast size of the Empire made the consolidation of power in the hands of the emperor very difficult and helps explain the Empire's decentralized structure.

The ties that bound the different members of the Empire to the emperor and also, though less strongly, to one another were of different origins, both old and new. Even in the early modern period, the Empire was first of all a feudal, hierarchical polity, with the emperor at its top. The feudal system was the bedrock of the medieval Empire's authority and property rights. It was based on a fundamental social exchange: a lord granted his vassal land, lordship rights, public offices, benefices, properties, and various dignities in exchange for personal fealty. The vassal committed himself wholly to advancing the well-being of his lord and protecting him physically, if needed; he owed his lord advice and assistance at all times. These feudal ties existed between free persons at all levels of society, from the emperor at the top down to the Common Man at the bottom, and they endured throughout the early modern period. As a feudal system, the Empire consisted of the sum total of all such fealty ties: it was an association in which all Imperial members (as well as many other persons) were immediate vassals of the emperor. This had the consequence that at the death of an emperor or any of his vassals, the feudal relationship had to be renewed through an act of solemn investiture, during which the emperor enfeoffed the vassal with his property and rights while the latter swore fealty to the emperor and the Empire. In the early modern period, this system began to erode as princes increasingly refrained from participating in Imperial rituals in person, sending instead proxies to the emperor's court. The nexus of the emperor's feudal ties extended to many Italian princes, and these ties did not subside but rather intensified in the wake of the Peace of Westphalia in 1648. In that respect, many Italian principalities continued to belong to the Empire even in the early modern period. (They were known as *Reichsitalien*, or Imperial Italy.) And yet, by the end of the Middle Ages, not all of the ties—not even most of them—between the emperor and other Imperial members were feudal in nature. A case in point is that of the Imperial cities: they related to the emperor not as vassals but as subjects.

Indeed, the Empire was never just a collection of feudal ties. It was also an association of members who shared a concrete set of institutions that evolved around 1500: the Imperial diets in their role as organs of common deliberation; the Imperial courts of law; and the Imperial circles (districts) in their function as regional executive organizations. According to such institutional (rather than feudal) logic, Imperial members were all those who possessed a seat and a vote at the Imperial diet and participated in the deliberation and common decision-making processes of that body; paid Imperial taxes to the emperor; made use of the Imperial courts of justice; and belonged to an Imperial circle. In other words, the Empire was a legal association under common juridical authority and with common legislative powers. It was a community of peace whose members, at least in theory, were supposed to stand by one another, avoid violent conflict, and pursue their shared financial and political aims by raising the community's own taxes and creating its own governmental organs. Nevertheless, not all Imperial members participated in these institutions to the same extent. Participation was a matter of concrete practices, and these were often contested and always changeable. Especially along the fringes of the Empire, there were members with contested or only weakly pronounced connections to it, including members whose ties to the Empire would be completely severed over time. But while the early modern Empire's fabric was slowly fraying, its center consisted of a group whose membership in it was never in doubt and who took part in all its common institutions, even if they did not always follow their decisions in practice. Even among these members, however, one could find some who were especially dependent on the emperor and the Empire—for instance, in the fragmented political landscape of Franconia, Swabia, and along the Middle Rhine, where the emperor's personal possessions had been located during the Middle Ages. The opposite was also true: many Imperial members in the north and northeast were physically distant from the emperor. Their attachment to him or to the Imperial institutions was consequently much weaker.

For all these reasons, it is not always easy to answer the question of who belonged to the Empire and who did not. A search for the exact physical boundaries of the Empire can be similarly frustrating. Some Imperial members belonged to the Empire in one sense but not in another—it all depends on the criteria one uses in judging such questions. As already mentioned, many principalities and urban communes in northern Italy—Tuscany, Mantua, Modena, Parma, Genoa, and Lucca—were bound by feudal ties to the Holy Roman Emperor, but otherwise took no part in any of the general Imperial institutions. (The important exception was the duchy of Savoy, which was a member of the Upper Rhenish Imperial circle and also had a seat and a vote in the Imperial diet.) In the wake of its successful revolt against its territorial rulers, the Habsburgs, the Swiss Confederation withdrew from all Imperial institutions, but remained de jure part of the Holy Roman Empire until the emperor recognized its formal independence in the Peace of Westphalia. Even after 1648, however, one must distinguish carefully between different members of the Swiss Confederation, which was anything but a homogeneous body. Indeed, some Swiss cantons continued to be formal vassals of the emperor until the dissolution of the Empire in

1806, highlighting their symbolic connections to him whenever it was politically expedient.

The Netherlands resembled the Swiss case in that different members of this political conglomeration maintained different degrees of connection to the Empire, although most conserved the feudal ties to the emperor. Ever since the late fifteenth century, the Low Countries were part of the Burgundian inheritance of the Habsburg dynasty and as such resisted any French claims to rule over them. Nevertheless, the Burgundian Treaty of 1548 severed most of their connections to the central Imperial institutions, and in 1555 they passed to the control of the Spanish branch of the Habsburg dynasty. When, during the age of confessional conflict following the Reformation, thirteen of the northern provinces formed an independent political union and started to wage a long war against their Catholic Spanish overlords, the Holy Roman Empire was no longer involved in the conflict. Thus, in 1648 the Republic of the United Provinces could assert its complete sovereignty on the international level. The southern provinces of the Netherlands (roughly, modern-day Belgium) remained under the rule of the Spanish Habsburgs but reverted back to the Austrian branch of the dynasty in 1713. Even then, however, they no longer belonged to the Holy Roman Empire in the strict sense of the term, because they possessed no seat and vote in the Imperial diet, paid no Imperial taxes, and did not place themselves under the jurisdiction of the Imperial courts.

Along the western borders of the Empire we find yet another example of the same complexity. Here, many territories continued to recognize the emperor as their feudal lord and even had the status of Imperial estates while also increasingly falling victim to France's expansionist policies. This is what happened, for instance, to the free county of Burgundy (Franche-Comté), the bishoprics of Metz, Toul, and Verdun, and the Imperial city of Strasbourg. The duchy of Lorraine oscillated for a long time between France, the Holy Roman Empire, and an independent, sovereign status. In fact, because of several small territories under his control, the duke of Lorraine continued to have a seat and a vote in the Imperial diet and other Imperial institutions even after his duchy had become, both de facto and de jure, part of France. Some northern territories continued to belong to the Empire even though their feudal ties connected them to monarchs outside of it. The king of Denmark, for instance, was also duke of Holstein, which undoubtedly belonged to the Empire; nearby Schleswig, on the other hand, a fief of the Danish king, did not belong to the Empire, although it was traditionally connected to Holstein. The Peace of Westphalia promised Western Pomerania to the king of Sweden without, however, loosening the province's ties to the Empire. Just like his Danish counterpart, the Swedish king possessed from that time on a seat and a vote in the Imperial diet. The duchy of Prussia, which until the beginning of the sixteenth century was ruled by the Teutonic Knights, had formed at different points in its history feudal ties both to Poland and to the Holy Roman Empire. During the Reformation, Albert, the Grand Master of the Teutonic Knights, secularized the duchy, and from then on it was a fief of the Polish crown, not the emperor. But in 1618, the elector of Brandenburg inherited the duchy and became, along with his many other titles, duke of Prussia. Forty years later, he even managed to assert his complete independence from Poland and consequently became a sovereign prince in this territory, a state of affairs that allowed his successor to claim for himself the title of "king in Prussia" in 1701. The final example is the kingdom of Bohemia. The king of Bohemia had been a vassal of the emperor since the Middle Ages and even acquired the status of an Imperial elector in the fourteenth century. But his Imperial fief consisted of his electoral office alone, not in the kingdom of Bohemia as such, which was also connected with Moravia, Silesia, and Lusatia. The king was a sovereign prince, and his lands did not stand under Imperial jurisdiction—that is, after 1500 they were not affected by the newly established Imperial institutions. After 1526, the Austrian branch of the Habsburg family also possessed the Bohemian crown, which meant that the king of Bohemia and the emperor were essentially one and the same person. For that reason, Bohemia was eventually incorporated more tightly into the Holy Roman Empire, a process completed in the early eighteenth century.

So much for the fringes. At the heart of the Empire stood the Imperial diet. The diet was an outgrowth of the king's great council (*Hoftag*), which acquired more stable institutional forms in the late Middle Ages (see pp. 54–57). Whoever had a seat and a vote in this assembly was an "Imperial estate," and thus unquestionably an Imperial member. (As with its German equivalent *Stand*, the original meaning of the English word "estate" was "standing or status.") One can divide the Imperial estates into three groups, according to the three main decision-making bodies (called *Kurien*, or *Räte*) in the Imperial diet in which they were members: the chamber of the electors; the chamber of the Imperial princes, counts, barons, and prelates; and the chamber of the Imperial cities. The Imperial knights had a separate status in this respect. Although they were Imperial members (that is, they enjoyed Imperial immediacy), they had neither seat nor vote in the Imperial diet. Let us look more closely at these groups one by one.

It was common to call the Imperial electors the columns on which the Imperial structure rested. They alone elected the emperor or the Roman king. Already in the Middle Ages, they formed a close corporation—an operative unit with common rights and privileges. They represented the Empire *pars pro toto* in the sense that their actions and decisions (as a group) claimed to be binding for the Empire as a whole. Ritually, too, their actions were enormously important. Their solemn appearance, together with the emperor's, made visible the majesty of the Empire as such. It is for that reason that many images of the Empire depict only the emperor and the electors.

The election of a medieval king was originally the business of the entire *populus*—that is, all potentates—but during the High Middle

Ages a smaller group managed to slowly assert its monopoly over the process. This group eventually included the three Rhenish archbishops of Mainz, Cologne, and Trier, as well as the king of Bohemia, the count Palatine of the Rhine, the duke of Saxony, and the margrave of Brandenburg. Even today, medievalists debate why it was these princes and not others who eventually attained the status of electors. Long after the process was complete, some scholars tried to legitimize retrospectively the elevated status of the four temporal electors through the so-called theory of the arch-offices (*Erzämtertheorie*). According to this theory, the four temporal Imperial electors had originally occupied the crucial ceremonial offices of cupbearer, seneschal, marshal, and chamberlain at the medieval king's court. Nevertheless, modern historians have demonstrated that the ceremonial offices were not the cause of the four temporal electors' elevated status but rather its consequence. Be that as it may, the Golden Bull issued by Emperor Charles IV in 1356 firmly established the seven-member group as a corporation with its distinct privileges, and on that basis it became the center of the Imperial political order and the nucleus around which the Imperial diet would later crystallize.

The Golden Bull (which by the sixteenth century had acquired the status of an Imperial fundamental law) laid down clear procedures for the election of a new Roman king, guaranteeing that, unlike in the past, the result of the process would be unambiguous and contested elections all but impossible. Especially important in this regard was the application of the primogeniture principle to the succession of the four temporal electorates. With such territories no longer divided among several sons at the death of an elector, the territorial integrity of each electorate, as well as the electors' total number, became much more stable. The Golden Bull also clarified many unresolved questions of rank and precedence among the Imperial electors that, because of the character of premodern society, had been the source of many conflicts in the past. This is why the

** Romischer Keyserlicher Ma-**
iestat Ordnung vnd Reformacion güter Pol-
licei im Heyligen Römischen Reich
Anno M. D. xxx. zu Aug-
spurgk auffgericht.

Cum gracia et Priuilegio Imperiali.

Figure 3. The Holy Roman emperor surrounded by the electors.
Print from 1531. *Source*: Paul Hoffmann, *Die bildlichen Darstellungen des Kurfürstenkollegiums von den Anfängen bis zum Ende des Heiligen Römischen Reiches (13.–18. Jahrhundert)*, Bonn, 1982, no. 37.

Golden Bull paid so much attention to the exact order in which the electors marched, stood, or sat during Imperial rituals. The Golden Bull further stipulated that the electors had the unique privilege to call themselves into session and that, even more important, the majority opinion would prevail in their deliberations. Such a decision-making procedure was unusual in premodern societies because it presupposed that votes could be counted accurately in the first place. After all, premodern societies were hierarchical systems in which *who* voiced an opinion far outweighed *how many* did so. The principle of decision-making by majority vote also relied on the fiction that the will of the majority was synonymous with the will of all. This stood in stark contrast to the typical premodern legitimization practices, which emphasized decision by consensus (*unanimitas*).

Despite the careful provisions of the Golden Bull, the composition of the chamber of electors did change over the course of the early modern period. The emperor outlawed the Palatine elector during the Thirty Years' War, transferring the dignity of his electorate in 1623 to the duke of Bavaria, who supported the emperor during the war. Nevertheless, when the Peace of Westphalia reestablished the Palatine electorate in 1648, the Bavarian duke retained his status, which increased the number of Imperial electors from seven to eight. When a Wittelsbach ruler united the Palatinate and Bavaria in 1777, the number of electors was reduced again. The duke of Braunschweig-Lüneburg also strove to acquire the status of an Imperial elector and even managed to do so in 1692, when the emperor granted it to him in exchange for a long list of political concessions. The Imperial diet recognized this development in 1708. Finally, in 1803, shortly before the dissolution of the Empire, the chamber of electors underwent one last fundamental (if also short-lived) transformation. The electoral status of the archbishops of Cologne and Trier was abolished, that of Mainz was transferred to Regensburg-Aschaffenburg, and new electorates were created for Württemberg, Hesse-Kassel, Baden, and Salzburg. Since the Empire ceased to exist only three years later, this transformation meant little in practice. Throughout the early modern period, the king of Bohemia played a particular role in the chamber of electors. As mentioned before, the Habsburg emperor and the king of Bohemia were essentially one and the same person, but Bohemia was not under the jurisdiction of the general Imperial institutions: its ruler, as king of Bohemia, paid no Imperial taxes and had no voting rights in the Imperial diet or any other Imperial institution. Only in 1708 did the emperor succeed in forcing his way as king of Bohemia into all the Imperial institutions. From that point on, Bohemia, too, possessed a seat and a vote in the Imperial diet.

The importance and prestige of an electoral status remained unchanged throughout the early modern period. It mattered little that after 1438 the chamber of electors almost always chose a member of the Habsburg dynasty to the Imperial throne. The exceptions were Charles VII, who was a Wittelsbach (see pp. 123–124), and Francis Stephen of Lorraine, who was elected in 1745 because of his status as the spouse of Maria Theresa, the daughter of the Habsburg emperor Charles VI (see p. 124). In the early modern period, it was common to elect the son (or, as in the case of Ferdinand I, the brother) of a reigning emperor as Roman king while the old emperor still lived (*vivente imperatore*). In this way, the uncertainties of an interregnum could be avoided and a dynastic continuity secured despite the electoral principle.

The importance of the electoral principle in the Empire rested, among other things, on the ability of the Imperial electors to dictate through it certain conditions to the soon-to-be king or emperor. This they did, beginning in 1519, in a document known as the "electoral capitulation" (*Wahlkapitulation*). This document was one of the most important elements in Imperial law (the Empire's *leges fundamentales*), though emperors often defied it in practice. The capitulation was essentially a political contract between monarch and estates in which both sides agreed to follow certain stipulations. Such negotiated contracts were typical of the limited monarchies of pre-modern times. The electoral capitulations amounted to a long inventory of the emperor's legal obligations vis-à-vis the Imperial estates; new items were added to this list cumulatively and unsystematically over time. It served the electors as a written guarantee that the emperor would keep intact all the electors' rights, liberties, and privileges (as well as those of other Imperial estates) and that he would seek their advice and consent regarding all major matters pertaining to the Empire as a whole. Attempts by non-electors to participate in the formulation of the capitulations proved unsuccessful, as did a movement to set these capitulations in stone once and for all.

Some Imperial electors played an important political role in the Empire above and beyond their electoral functions. The Palatine elector and his Saxon counterpart occupied the offices of Imperial vicars in the eastern and western parts of the Empire, respectively. In these roles, they represented the king during an interregnum and enjoyed substantive income. The three ecclesiastical electors served as archchancellors in the Empire's three main parts: the archbishop of Mainz in Germany, the archbishop of Cologne in Italy, and the archbishop of Trier in Gaul (Lorraine and Burgundy). During the early modern period, when political activity in the Empire was concentrated more and more in its German-speaking parts, the elector of Mainz acquired an especially important position, that of Imperial archchancellor. He was the highest-ranking of all Imperial members and as such enjoyed a prominent position whenever the Empire functioned as an organization separate from the person of the emperor. Most importantly, he organized Imperial diets, led the election of a new king, and even crowned and anointed the king/emperor in Frankfurt am Main (a privilege he managed to definitively wrestle from the archbishop of Cologne during the early modern period). The Imperial Aulic chancellery (*Reichshofkanzlei*) was the center of legal communication in the Empire and, strictly speaking, an organ of the Imperial archchancellor (the archbishop of Mainz).

Nevertheless, well into the seventeenth century it retained important responsibilities regarding the territories under direct Habsburg control. As such, it had its seat in the emperor's court and was led in its daily business by the Imperial vice chancellor rather than the Imperial archchancellor. To what extent the Reichshofkanzlei was an instrument of the Imperial archchancellor and not the emperor depended largely on the person who headed the office at any given time. Some archbishops of Mainz—for instance, Berthold von Henneberg at the end of the fifteenth century or John Philip in the seventeenth century—were important political counterweights to the emperor and managed to shape Imperial politics independently of him.

Overall, the chamber of electors was of great constitutional and political importance in the Empire, especially when the emperor withdrew himself from Imperial affairs—which happened, for instance, in the fifteenth century—or when other Imperial organs ceased to function, as was the case on the eve of and during the Thirty Years' War. Only in the wake of the Peace of Westphalia, when several of the Imperial electors ascended to royal crowns outside the Empire and consequently acquired much more political power than others, did the chamber lose some of its importance. These were the Imperial elector of Brandenburg, who crowned himself king in Prussia in 1701; the Imperial elector of Saxony, who was elected king of Poland in 1697; and the Imperial elector of Braunschweig, who became king of Great Britain in 1714.

The Imperial electors formed the first and most important of the Imperial diet's three chambers. The second consisted of other Imperial princes, prelates, counts, and barons. Whereas the chamber of electors had formed a closed and relatively homogeneous corporation ever since the fourteenth century, nothing of the sort can be said about the diet's second chamber, which over the course of the early modern period consisted of a fluctuating number of members with diverse social ranks and unequal political weights.

A first group in this second chamber consisted of temporal and ecclesiastical princes. Already in the High Middle Ages, Imperial princes managed to close their ranks to new arrivals from below; only a very few ordinary noble families (for example, the house of Württemberg) managed to acquire the status of Imperial princes. This group possessed important political and legal privileges, including legal jurisdiction in their territories, toll and minting privileges, and ecclesiastical guardianships. In other words, they were in control of all those elements that could form the nucleus of a future fully territorial lordship (*dominium terrae*). Imperial princes were direct vassals of the emperor, and they were lords in turn of their own vassals both within and outside their territories. Each of them had an individual seat and vote in the Imperial diet (*Virilstimmen*), a vestige of their old right as vassals of the emperor to give him counsel and assistance. They nevertheless varied considerably in their political power, as well as in the size and number of the territories each had under his control.

The temporal Imperial princes received their lands by inheritance, regardless of the ritual of enfeoffment by the emperor. Next to them were also the ecclesiastical Imperial princes, who, in addition to the ecclesiastical offices they occupied (as archbishops, bishops, abbots, and abbesses), were also lords of temporalities (secular territorial possessions) known in German as *Hochstifte*. This meant in practice that the organization of the Church in the Empire (also known as the Imperial church, or Reichskirche) was closely intertwined with the latter's political and social order. Under canon law, holders of ecclesiastical offices were elected by their cathedral chapters or, in abbeys, by the monks or nuns before being confirmed by the pope. As rulers of temporalities, however, ecclesiastical Imperial princes were vassals of the emperor and received their territories from him. In the early modern period, the Empire's ecclesiastical princes often came from a region's lower or middling nobility (for example, members of the important Schönborn family), although some were from the great princely dynasties. If elected bishop or archbishop, a member of the lower nobility could attain the rank of an Imperial prince, or even that of an elector, although he did not belong to that group by birth. In the aftermath of the Reformation, the election of the ecclesiastical Imperial princes became an especially explosive political issue that no one wanted to leave to the care of the cathedral chapters or the abbeys alone. The emperor, the electors, the Imperial princes, and even foreign powers exerted much pressure on the elective bodies (for example, through various "presents") in order to influence the outcome of elections. Even the pope was not above the fray in this respect, giving generous dispensation from canon law when political expediency demanded it—for instance, when the most convenient candidate was still a minor, or someone who refused to leave another ecclesiastical office. Inasmuch as they did not disappear in the secularization of church property that followed the Reformation, the highest positions in the Imperial church served as important political tools in the emperor's hands. They were pawns in the larger patron-client system through which the Habsburgs maintained their control in the Empire.

The number of temporal and ecclesiastical princes with a seat and a vote in the early modern Imperial diet was never stable. The Imperial tax register of the diet of Worms (Wormser Matrikel, 1521)—an imperfect list of taxpaying Imperial members whose accuracy is hotly debated by modern historians—mentions four archbishops, forty-six bishops, and twenty-four princes. In the wake of the Reformation, many princes secularized Imperial bishoprics or, in a process known as "mediatization," incorporated them into their territories (thus robbing them of Imperial immediacy). This development reduced the number of ecclesiastical Imperial territories by about half. The number of temporal Imperial territories, on the other hand, increased over the course of the early modern period to about sixty, partly because of the transformation of many ecclesiastical territories into temporal ones when the emperor decided to enlarge his clientele pool by raising some territories to the rank of an Imperial estate. From the seventeenth century onward, however, the admission of newly minted Imperial princes to the diet depended on the consent of the electors and the existing group of Imperial princes; as a result, few actually managed to claim a seat in the diet's second chamber. A century earlier, the progressive fragmentation of noble territories through inheritance by more than one son had increased the number of temporal princes. In 1582, the Imperial diet put a stop to this process by binding a seat and a vote in the diet to the territory itself. If a noble family had more than one son and partitioned its territory among them, the new lords would still control only one (common) seat in the Imperial diet. Some Imperial principalities severed their ties to the Empire completely around this time. This was the case with the ecclesiastical Imperial territories of Metz, Toul, and Verdun, which, following the Peace of Westphalia, fell to France.

Next to the Imperial princes, the Imperial diet also included middling Imperial estates whose members did not possess an individual seat and vote in the diet. Instead, they built "benches" (*Bänke*) through which they exercised a collective vote (*Kuriatstimme*). These members possessed only limited political power, and their social rank was also relatively low. Indeed, some of them lacked the means to represent themselves in the diet at all. Typical members of this group were the Imperial prelates, on the one hand, and the counts and barons (*Grafen und Freiherren*), on the other hand. As individuals, these persons had little political power, but as a collective group and in their sheer numbers they shaped the character of the Empire to a considerable degree.

Just like prince-bishops, heads of Imperial abbeys and collegiate churches enjoyed the rights of territorial authority in their own domains. Even women could exercise such lordship powers, as abbesses. These Imperial prelates combined to create two more benches in the diet—the Swabian and Rhenish prelate benches, respectively. The Imperial tax register of the diet of Worms mentions eighty-three prelates, fourteen of them women. For exactly the same reason the number of Imperial ecclesiastical princes declined—secularization and mediatization—the number of Imperial prelates also decreased sharply in the course of the early modern period, to about two-thirds of its early sixteenth-century strength. The prelates' territories— middling Imperial estates on which the emperor relied heavily— were concentrated in the Empire's southwest. In terms of its social composition, the Imperial church was always a nobles' church: because of the wealth it controlled, the chapters of the Imperial bishoprics, the Imperial abbeys, and the ecclesiastical territories served especially the younger sons and daughters of a given region's local nobility.

Counts and barons belonged to the lowest group of the Imperial nobility. Such nobles controlled very small territories that failed to develop into anything resembling independent territorial states. Even in their own lands they did not enjoy full territorial authority, and indeed, some were vassals of neighboring princes. Their Imperial immediacy was consequently always precarious and often under attack by more powerful Imperial princes. Counts and barons sometimes managed to assert their independence from their greedy neighbors and pay taxes only to the emperor, but they remained dependent on their confessionally like-minded and more powerful neighbors in many respects, occupying important positions in the latter's courts and orienting their behavior according to foreign political interests. This characterized, for example, the mutual relationships between the Wetterau Imperial counts and the Palatine electors, between the northern German counts and electoral Saxony, and between the Swabian lower nobility and the Habsburg emperors.

By the late Middle Ages, most Imperial barons had already been raised to the rank of Imperial counts. During the early modern period, there was consequently little practical difference between these two groups. A handful of such nobles appeared in person in the Imperial diets, but if only for financial reasons, they could not attend the diet on a regular basis. To finance and coordinate a common representation in the diet as well as to stage a common fight against attempts by powerful neighbors to rob them of their Imperial immediacy, the Imperial counts and barons were compelled to organize themselves along corporative lines, forming regional organizations with a common treasury and statutes, regular correspondence, and so on. This wasn't always easy. The oldest and most efficient of these organizations was the Wetterau association of Imperial counts; later, the Swabian counts established a similar association. Starting in 1524, both associations formed a bench together in the Imperial diet, each with its own independent, common vote. In 1640 an association of Franconian counts formed an additional bench in the diet, and in 1653 a lower Rhenish-Westphalian bench too was added. The Imperial tax register of the diet of Worms lists 143 individual counts and barons. In the course of the early modern period, about one-third of these families died out, and another third either lost their Imperial immediacy to a greedy neighbor or were among the lucky few families whom the emperor raised to the rank of Imperial princes. Many countships fell, by marriage or heritage, into the hands of the great princely dynasties, which severely weakened the solidarity between the remaining counts and barons. At the same time, the emperor raised many non-noble families to the rank of Imperial counts or barons, causing much tension between old and new Imperial counts. The old families built a group of important clients for the emperor and sustained themselves through service at the emperor's court and his army. Their continued status as immediate members of the Empire was completely dependent on their ties to the emperor; without his support and assistance, they would not have been able to maintain their political existence.

The third and final group represented in Imperial diets by a separate corporate body were the Imperial cities. In an important sense, they were a foreign communal element among the otherwise land-based aristocracy that dominated the Empire's body politic: a series of distinct, legally privileged spaces within an environment structured around the possession of land and feudal ties. The Imperial cities were autonomous communities of burghers (citizens of towns) who ruled themselves internally through a burgomaster and a city council and projected their authority outwardly in an almost aristocratic fashion—raising taxes, dispensing justice, and even establishing lordly forms of authority in their immediate geographic vicinity. The Imperial cities recognized the emperor alone as their lord, and they paid taxes to him only. In contradistinction to other more or less autonomous urban communities in the Empire, they managed to break away completely from the jurisdiction of neighboring lords. Some such cities had been the emperor's direct subjects since time immemorial: he was their direct feudal lord, and they owed taxes only to him. (Among these Imperial cities, in the strictest sense of the term, were Nuremberg, Ulm, and Frankfurt am Main.) Other so-called free cities had managed to free themselves from the control of a local lord over time (for example, Cologne, Speyer, and Regensburg). Cities that served as important textile and commercial centers, like Augsburg and Nuremberg, were of great importance to the emperor, who could skim off some of their wealth for his own purposes. It is important to emphasize in this respect that Imperial and free cities were not entitled to the same rights as noble vassals—the emperor was not obliged to reach a consensus with them on fundamental political, legal, and tax-related questions. They were entitled to discuss the terms under which they were to pay the emperor a certain amount. Their obligation to do so, however, was never in doubt.

The tax register of the diet of Worms lists eighty-five Imperial cities, but the exact legal status of many of them continued to be a bone of contention throughout the early modern period. The issue was whether such urban communities truly could claim political autonomy and Imperial immediacy or whether the local magnate in whose territory they were located had the right to incorporate them into his lands—as happened, for instance, with Braunschweig and Bremen. Some cities, such as Hamburg, managed to maneuver successfully between the two extremes for a very long time. The overall number of free and Imperial cities declined over the course of the early modern period by about 25 percent. Most of them were found in the western and southwestern parts of the Empire: in Franconia, Swabia, and Alsace, along the Middle Rhine, and in Westphalia. They were a heterogeneous group in terms of size and economic importance and included large and rich commercial centers like Ulm, Augsburg, Nuremberg, and Cologne, alongside tiny communes like Buchau in Swabia and Zell am Harmersbach near the Black Forest.

In 1471, the Imperial and free cities formed an organization with a corporative structure, including a special diet (*Städtetag*) in which they assembled regularly to defend their collective rights and discuss questions of common interest. After overcoming some early opposition to their role in the Imperial diet, the Imperial and free cities also constituted a deliberative body within the diet itself. This was the third of the diet's three chambers—the chamber of cities. Just like the Imperial counts and barons, the cities organized themselves into two benches—a Swabian one and a Rhenish one—at which individual delegates often represented more than one city. From the sixteenth century on, there was no question that the Imperial and free cities had to participate in all the major Imperial institutions. The only exception was the Imperial diet itself, in which cities' participation remained limited, largely because the two upper chambers often found common ground with the emperor without the cities' assistance and, even when that was not the case, did not recognize the right of the cities to participate fully in the diet's decision-making processes. Only in 1582 did the cities formally acquire this right— the *votum decisivum*—which the Peace of Westphalia later confirmed but which could never really be practiced.

The Imperial knights had a special position within the Empire's corporative structure. They were members of the lower nobility who lived in the Empire's southwest and who, as descendants of former holders of Imperial offices (*Reichsministerialen*), exercised limited juridical powers without becoming lords of actual territories (*Landesherren*). Though without lands of their own, the knights claimed Imperial immediacy and in the course of the sixteenth century managed to resist infringements on their rights by stronger lords. During the early modern period, they became quite distinct from the families of Imperial counts and barons, who refrained from forming marital ties with them. Despite the fact that the knights recognized no lord aside from the emperor, they did not take part in Imperial diets. The tax register of the diet of Worms does not mention them at all, and the institutions of the Imperial circles did not include them (see pp. 58–59).

Even more than the Imperial counts and barons, the knights were in a very precarious position during the transition period from the late Middle Ages to the early modern period. Their independent existence was in jeopardy because of the fundamental changes in military practice and the state-building processes in the Empire's large territories. To compensate for their reduced military role, as well as to resist attempts at mediatization by neighboring princes and lords, the knights created their own corporative organizations (for example, the Knightly Order of St. Jörgenschild). In 1542, in response to the emperor's demand that they contribute financially to the war against the Ottomans, the Imperial knights formed a collective body with the right to make their monetary contributions directly to the emperor (rather than to a territorial lord). Nevertheless, such contributions always remained voluntary (*Caritativsubsidien*), because the knights were not represented in the Imperial diet and consequently did not feel bound by its decisions. A general organization of all Imperial knights never came into being. Instead, there were fifteen knightly cantons (*Ritterkantone, Ritterorte*) which in turn formed three knightly circles (*Ritterkreise*)—Franconian, Swabian, and Rhenish. In the early modern period, these organizations were able to compensate somewhat for the political weaknesses of the individual Imperial knights. Like the Imperial counts, the knights also formed an important subgroup within the totality of the emperor's clients. Over time, some families of knightly origin managed to climb the Imperial ladder and reach some of the highest positions in the service of the emperor and the Imperial church. One prominent example in this respect is the Schönborn family, several members of which became Imperial abbots and even electors.

One final curiosity of the Imperial constitution was the case of the Imperial villages. These were peasant communities with limited political autonomy that had managed to assert their Imperial immediacy against mediatization attempts ever since the Middle Ages. In the early modern period, the Imperial villages, even more so than the Imperial knights, were little more than anachronistic relics— medieval islands in a modern sea of transformative state-building processes. Indeed, in 1803, only five such communities were still in existence. The great German romantic writer Jean Paul immortalized them in his novel *Siebenkäs* (published in three volumes, 1796–1797), a satire about the fictitious Imperial village of Kuhschnappel. Satire aside, the Imperial villages exemplified a fundamental aspect of Imperial law: new structures never completely subsumed old ones.

3

INSTITUTIONAL CONSOLIDATION, 1495–1521

By the late Middle Ages, the Holy Roman Empire resembled "a network of leading families' interests" (Peter Moraw) more than a closed political community. But in the fifteenth century, internal structural problems and external conflicts strengthened the need for cooperation among Imperial members and led to the emergence of a new, durable, and resilient set of Imperial institutions.

The fifteenth century witnessed a series of fundamental socioeconomic changes across central Europe. Everywhere, previously separate markets became more tightly integrated and formerly distinct financial networks became more closely intertwined. Many cities in southern and central Germany, whose economy was increasingly tied to mining, metalwork, and textile production, evolved into early centers of commercial capitalism. Accelerating these changes was the development of new forms of military fortification and the rising power of the artillery. Instead of relying on armored knights, as in the past, early modern rulers depended more and more on a rising class of military entrepreneurs who offered them troops for hire from all echelons of society. Thus, the money economy began to dominate even the way war was waged. Finally, the reception of late antique Roman law contributed to a slow professionalization of judges and princely councilors.

No social group suffered more from the developments of the fifteenth century than the lower nobility—the counts and especially the knights. Many a great lord actually profited from these developments, because they facilitated the expansion of princely territories. The knights, on the other hand, insisted on using violence in pursuing what they considered to be their inalienable rights. The result was a growing public concern about the armed conflicts carried on by members of the lower nobility, a problem exacerbated by the fact that, unlike modern states, the Empire did not claim a monopoly over the use of violence within its borders. Because of the growing integration of markets, it was important to protect commercial routes and safeguard the reliability of the coin and credit systems, but these tasks were beyond the means of individual lords. To contemporaries, the protection of law and order was above all the emperor's responsibility; they consequently understood the structural problems in the Empire as primarily a problem of the decreasing power of an emperor who often resided outside the Empire itself. All these considerations led to a growing consensus among Imperial members about the need for more cooperation.

Beyond internal developments, it was also a series of external threats that brought about a closer cooperation between different Imperial estates: the Hussite Wars of the early fifteenth century; the constant threat, ever since the fall of Constantinople in 1453, of an Ottoman invasion of southeastern Europe; the war against Matthias Corvinus, king of Hungary, who managed to occupy Vienna in 1485; the impact on Germany's western provinces of the Hundred Years' War between England and France; the wars against Charles the Bold, the ambitious duke of Burgundy; and the French invasion of northern Italy in 1494. The growing preference for hiring troops for cash rather than employing feudal, land-based forms of military recruitment made waging war increasingly more expensive. Unlike in previous centuries, by the fifteenth century the emperor possessed no crown or Imperial revenues with which to support his role as supreme warlord. He could not raise taxes in the Empire unilaterally because, legally speaking, raising taxes was an exception rather than a rule. As such, the emperor couldn't simply raise taxes from the Imperial members—he had to make a formal request to at least the more powerful among them. The military conflicts of the fifteenth century made the situation even worse. The emperor had no choice but to request extraordinary taxes from *all* Imperial members, but he could do so only once it became clear who was such a member and who wasn't.

The need for closer cooperation between different Imperial estates was also the result of the special position of the Habsburg emperors. Because the gravitational center of the Habsburg dynasty lay in the southeastern periphery of the Empire, emperors often ruled the Empire from afar (the best example being the fifty-year reign of Emperor Frederick III). Consequently, during the fifteenth century it was common for Imperial meetings to take place with the Imperial electors and sometimes other Imperial members present, but without an emperor who could help them reach a common decision. At the same time, the constant possibility of conflict within the Empire and along its borders strengthened the need for cooperation between Imperial members. The result of all this was not only more stable procedural forms in Imperial meetings but also an understanding among many in the Empire that all Imperial members shared common goals and interests and that indeed they all belonged to the same polity. Despite the failure of previous attempts to reform the Imperial institutions, it slowly became clear that such reform was the order of the day. Indeed, several important scholars had been raising this issue ever since the early fifteenth century, especially in relation to the parallel attempts to reform the Catholic Church in the councils of Constance (1414–1418) and Basel (1431–1449).

One cannot understand the reform of the Imperial institutions—which was finally accomplished around 1500—outside the context of the simultaneous, decisive concentration of power in the hands of the Habsburgs. Emperor Frederick III died in 1493. His successor was his son Maximilian, who had already married the daughter and heir of Charles the Bold in 1477 and had been elected Roman king in 1486. Maximilian quickly lost the heartland of Charles the Bold's realm—Burgundy itself—but he successfully defended another part of his father-in-law's lands that was actually larger and more important than Burgundy itself: the extremely rich, densely populated, highly urbanized, and economically advanced Low Countries. Another crucial chess move on Maximilian's part was the marriage of his son, Philip the Fair, to Johanna, daughter of the Spanish royal pair Isabella of Castile and Ferdinand of Aragon. Because other possible heirs had passed away, the Habsburgs eventually inherited both Spanish crowns and, what is more, the new Spanish acquisitions in the New World. In the early sixteenth century, another successful marriage secured the kingdom of Bohemia and so this land, too, came under Habsburg control. Thus, by the sixteenth century, the Habsburgs had gained unprecedented control over substantial parts of Europe, and indeed the world.

When he ascended to the Imperial throne in 1493, Emperor Maximilian I brought to the office his earlier experience in the Low Countries: the extravagant ceremonials of lordship he had witnessed growing up in Burgundy, modern forms of military conscription and artillery, and novel ways of administering finances. An important side effect of the supra-regional concentration of power in the hands of the Habsburgs was the introduction and spread of the post system, which allowed the Habsburgs to control their widespread territories and especially the financial centers in northern Italy, southern Germany, the Low Countries, and Spain. The decisive innovative aspect of this system was the creation of postal stations where riders could change horses quickly, thus accelerating the speed with which they spread information. To consolidate the system further, Maximilian granted a monopoly over the post system to the noble family of Thurn and Taxis, which, in turn, made the system available to almost anyone by creating a system of fixed routes, timetables, and prices. The Imperial post system, together with the ever wider use of the printing press, brought about a veritable revolution in communication in the Empire and across Europe.

Maximilian I's rule set the stage for the structural evolution of the Empire in the following three hundred years. Many historians speak in this regard about a "period of Imperial reform," but this expression can be misleading. "Reform" (*reformatio* in Latin) did not have the same connotation in the early modern period as it does today: originally, it denoted a return to the "good old order" rather than a programmatic attempt to shape the future. Moreover, the use of the singular obscures the fact that the political actions of the advocates of Imperial reform around 1500 did not amount to a synchronized, carefully planned attempt to reach a common goal. Rather, their actions were pragmatic reactions to specific problems and challenges (all in the plural); reformers were making repeated attempts to seek political compromises for particular issues. It was through this process, and not through a carefully laid-out plan, that truly new, future-oriented forms of political structures emerged.

The reform measures reoriented Imperial institutions toward more stable forms and a greater emphasis on the rule of law. Even after the reforms of Maximilian's time, different Imperial members continued to pursue their individual and at times conflicting interests. But unlike earlier times, they did so now while also working together with other members on the level of the Empire as a whole and through a relatively stable set of institutions. Symptomatic of this development was the fact that *Reich*, the German term for "empire," underwent an important semantic transformation around this time. During the Middle Ages, its meaning was ambiguous and could denote, among other things, the very office of the emperor.

After the late fifteenth century, however, *Reich* became associated more and more with the sum total of all the Imperial estates, with or without the Emperor, an indication that the Empire possessed stable enough institutions that it could now be conceived as separate from the actual person of the emperor (hence the common formulation, dating back to this time, of *Kaiser und Reich*, "emperor *and* Empire"). The Imperial diet of Worms in 1495 represented the high point of this semantic stabilization process. It was the first meeting of Imperial members for which the sources use the term "Imperial diet" (Reichstag), an indication that it was no longer the traditional court meeting to which emperors called only their vassals and trusted followers. Berthold von Henneberg, archbishop of Mainz and Imperial archchancellor, exerted decisive influence on the laws promulgated at the Imperial diet of 1495. We cannot know for sure whether or not Henneberg developed a clear reform platform for the diet, but it is likely that he did follow a political strategy there, supported by all participants and aimed at solving the structural problems of the Empire once and for all. Compared with modern political reform movements, Henneberg's political platform seems limited; compared with similar attempts to reform the Empire both before and after him, however, it was remarkably coherent.

The concrete incentive for the 1495 Imperial diet of Worms was the ascension of Maximilian I to the Imperial throne two years earlier. This was the first general estates' assembly of the new king, and according to the medieval tradition, such an assembly carried a special weight. It was the custom in such a meeting for many electors and other princes to come see the emperor in person, to celebrate his rule with much pomp and circumstance, and to have him enfeoff them. It was also customary in the first general assembly of an emperor for Imperial members to stage their own spectacles of lordship, complete with their own retinues, and to give counsel to the new king or emperor about pressing political issues. Different participants at the diet of Worms pursued distinct political goals. The new emperor sought the consent of the Imperial estates for raising revenues to help him repulse the Ottoman Turks in the southeast as well as the French in Italy. He acted, however, as if he were in a commanding position vis-à-vis the estates and regarded them almost as if they were supplicants at his personal court. The estates, for their part, demanded to have their opinions count in matters concerning the Empire if they were to provide the emperor with money. The impulses for Imperial reform came consequently from two directions: from an emperor who was in dire need of money for his many military campaigns; and from the Imperial estates, who sought to solve the common structural problems afflicting the Empire and demanded to have a say in such matters from now on. From its very inception, the issue of Imperial reform was consequently characterized by structural tensions. On the one hand was a generally felt need for central regulation, unachievable without the participation of the Imperial estates; on the other hand, Imperial members (and especially the more powerful among them) had their own particular interests that were not necessarily aligned with the political aims of all the others, let alone those of the emperor. Thus, as they pursued their own interest, many Imperial members supported the "Imperial reform movement" only halfheartedly.

After long negotiations, many difficulties, and many compromises, the 1495 Imperial diet of Worms did manage to reach a series of related reform laws. Berthold von Henneberg's role in coordinating this process was crucial. The most fundamental law the diet reached was the so-called perpetual public peace (Ewiger Landfrieden): the general and permanent prohibition on any form of blood feud in the Empire. This was a novel development, because similar agreements in the past had always been either related to specific conflicts or limited in time. Pursuing one's rights by violent means, a formerly legally sanctioned way to handle political disputes (and not only among nobles), was now explicitly banned. In practice, this was a step toward the concentration of the legitimate use of violence in the hands of the Empire's great territorial lords, who could still use coercive methods in their role as supreme judges in their own individual lands.

Banning blood feuds alone, however, was not enough. To secure the public peace, it was also imperative to create a legal framework that would allow for the resolution of political conflicts without the use of violence. This was the motivation behind the establishment of "the emperor's and Empire's chamber court" (Reichskammergericht), generally shortened to "Imperial chamber court." In both procedure and composition, the Imperial chamber court was a completely novel legal entity. At first glance, it looks like a modified version of the old chamber court of the emperor. In reality, however, it was much more than that, since the emperor, in his role as the supreme judge in the Empire, lost some of his powers to a judiciary dominated by the Imperial estates. A strong indication of this development was the very location of the court: throughout the early modern period, it remained far from the emperor's residence. At first, the Imperial chamber court convened in alternating places, but after 1527 it found a stable domicile in the free Imperial city of Speyer and then, after fleeing the advancing troops of Louis XIV in 1689, in Wetzlar, where it remained until the dissolution of the Empire in the early nineteenth century. The emperor exerted influence on the court by nominating its president (*Kammerrichter*). The actual judges, however, were not the presidents but the "assessors" (*Assessoren*, or *Schöffen*), who were nominated by the Imperial estates rather than the emperor. Guiding the election of assessors was a complicated and changing process that took into account both the estates involved and their physical location in the Empire. The emperor's advocate in the Imperial chamber court was known as the *Reichsfiskal*.

The Imperial chamber court's ordinance (which underwent substantial modifications in 1555 and 1654) determined a set number of noble judges and legally trained non-noble judges, and it prescribed a written legal procedure that was largely reliant on canon law. The court had a series of quite varied responsibilities. It served as a court of first instance for all conflicts between Imperial members, but it also heard cases that involved breaches of the public peace or the denial of legal access within princely territories. The Imperial chamber court could also serve as an appellate court: it could hear appeals of decisions by the supreme courts of individual Imperial lands, but only as long as the rulers of such lands did not possess the *privilegium de non appellando*—the princely privilege not to have one's courts' decisions appealed in courts outside of one's lands. The procedural rules of the Imperial chamber court were a decisive conduit in the spread of Roman law in the Holy Roman Empire and exerted a crucial influence on the professionalization and homogenization of judiciaries across Germany. They served as a model for the organization of all legal matters in the Empire's individual territories.

As a countermeasure for the establishment of the estates-dominated Imperial chamber court, Maximilian I issued a new set of rules for his old Imperial Aulic council (Reichshofrat). This council had been the emperor's central organ for handling governmental, feudal, and judicial matters and was furthermore the highest legal instance in the Habsburgs' hereditary lands as well as the Empire as a whole. The establishment of the Imperial chamber court was not accompanied by the dissolution of the Imperial Aulic council or by the drawing of clear demarcation lines between the two courts' legal spheres. By the early sixteenth century, consequently, there were two supreme appellate courts in the Empire, and they were often at odds with each other. As in the past, the Imperial Aulic council remained the principal organ of the emperor, whom all Imperial members continued to regard, at least in theory, as the supreme judge in the Empire and as such independent of the estates. Thus, all later attempts by individual Imperial estates to intervene in the procedures or composition of the Imperial Aulic council proved futile.

Moreover, throughout the early modern period the Imperial Aulic council remained by far the faster and more efficient of the two supreme Imperial courts. Even the estates themselves often acknowledged this fact by their preference for appealing to the Imperial Aulic council rather than the Imperial chamber court. The latter was so often torn by questions of confessional alliance that its work all but completely ground to a halt.

Despite the tensions that characterized their coexistence, the two Imperial courts exerted decisive influence on the Empire's constitution throughout the early modern period and contributed to the Empire's role as the general legal framework for all its members. They helped deal with a plethora of political, economic, social, and religious conflicts through legal proceedings rather than by force. All conceivable constellations were possible in this respect: Imperial members (and their subjects) suing one another, subjects bringing legal claims against their rulers, local estates seeking protection from their territorial rulers, and peasant communities taking legal actions against their local lords. Despite common early modern complaints about the courts' ponderousness and political dependencies, one should not underestimate their importance for the inner coherence of the Empire. It is true that legal proceedings did not always solve conflicts and that the different parties to a dispute (especially the more powerful among the Imperial estates) did not always respect the courts' verdicts in practice. Still, even in such cases, the fact that the issues were addressed by the courts helped to prevent other, more violent attempts to resolve them, at least for a while.

The Imperial chamber court needed a stable source of revenue. For that purpose, as well as a way to repay the emperor for his wars against the Ottomans, the Imperial diet agreed on a general Imperial tax—the so-called Common Penny (Gemeiner Pfennig)—which was initially set for a period of four years. The Common Penny stemmed from a very modern idea: all Imperial residents over the age of fifteen (both men and women!) were to pay this tax according to a coarse system of property brackets. The responsibility for collecting the tax fell on local parishes, and its administration was handled by an Imperial body specifically created for that purpose. This taxation system gave the Empire direct access to all of its residents, allowing it to circumvent the intermediary power of territorial lords. Indeed, had the Common Penny been successful, it could have facilitated the emergence of modern governmental structures on the level of the Empire as a whole. It was exactly for this reason, however, that the execution of the plan failed in practice—it was simply not in the interest of the great territorial lords for it to succeed. With the failure of the Common Penny, the raising of Imperial taxes remained for the rest of the early modern period in the hands of the Imperial estates. They went about doing so by first reaching a decision about a total sum to be raised in the Empire as a whole (a sum known as *Römermonate*), then apportioning it among themselves according to an agreement they laid down in the already mentioned tax register of the diet of Worms in 1521. From the moment of its inception, the agreement of 1521 was highly contested because it was not flexible enough to address the frequently changing financial circumstances of the Empire and could not be changed without the consent of the great Imperial lords, who, for their part, refused to modify an agreement that favored them. The Imperial estates managed to pass on the burden of Imperial taxes to their subjects; they did not pay them out of their own regular revenues. Consequently, the Empire never raised a general, direct tax from all its inhabitants and, at least in terms of taxation, never formed a unified body of Imperial subjects. Paradoxically, then, this taxation system ended up strengthening the taxation authority of the territorial lords rather than the Empire, because it allowed individual rulers to raise taxes from their subjects without the consent of territorial estates. (This consent had already been given by the *Imperial* estates.)

The emperor and the Imperial estates reached one final decision in the Imperial diet of Worms in 1495, the "Handling of Peace and

Law" (*Handhabung Friedens und Rechts*). This "handling" allowed for the permanent participation of the estates in Imperial politics through the annual calling of an Imperial diet and the need for the estates' consent in decisions about taxation and war and peace. This regulation did not prove successful. In retrospect, however, it did help to legitimize the proceedings and character of Imperial diets as they had already begun to emerge in the last quarter of the fifteenth century.

The procedural forms of Imperial diets finally crystallized in the sixteenth century. A diet began with the emperor inviting all Imperial estates to assemble in an Imperial city such as Regensburg, Nuremberg, Augsburg, Worms, or Speyer. The emperor did not send invitations himself. Rather, he had the Imperial archchancellor, the archbishop of Mainz, do so on his behalf. The diet opened with a Mass to the Holy Spirit, a ceremony that lent the following proceedings sacral authority. Then, in a first and solemn meeting of the diet attended either by the emperor in person or by his proxy, the assembled estates listened to the emperor's proposition, in which he prescribed the topics for common deliberation. In this first solemn meeting of the diet, contemporaries paid special attention to the exact seating arrangements, which were critically important because they mirrored in practice the abstract hierarchical order of the different Imperial estates. No wonder, therefore, that seating arrangements often gave cause for many heated disputes.

After its first meeting, the diet split into three chambers: those of the electors, the Imperial princes, and the Imperial cities. The emperor was absent from the deliberations in all three chambers, which proceeded individually to discuss the diet's agenda behind closed doors. The discussions in the individual chambers took place according to the following procedure: one by one, all members were asked to voice their opinion about a specific item on the agenda, and the rounds did not conclude before all participants had agreed on a common position. Counting votes or reaching a decision by majority vote was generally frowned upon; the basic principle of the deliberations was to reach a consensus, not a majority. Nevertheless, in the second half of the sixteenth century it became customary to record in writing the individual votes in all three chambers. Having concluded their separate conclaves, the first two chambers then exchanged the results of their deliberations and tried to correlate them with each other (*re-* and *correlation*) until they, too, reached a common position (*amicabilis compositio*). The first two chambers presented their common position to the chamber of the Imperial cities, whose decisive contribution to Imperial finances was by no means matched by its largely advisory position in the diet. Indeed, the system of deliberations in the diet made the voice of the electors worth as much as that of all other princes and cities put together; it gave them a far greater political weight than all other Imperial estates. Nonetheless, to facilitate the discussion of particular topics, it was also customary to form ad hoc committees and to draw their members from all three chambers. This practice broke with the principle of separate deliberation in the three chambers: all committee members had an equal vote in the deliberation, including the city representatives and even the Imperial prelates and counts. In the long run, the work of the Imperial diet's ad hoc committees failed exactly because of their diverse composition: the Imperial electors did not want to lose the political advantage they enjoyed in the diet's general deliberative system. Finally, the chambers presented the emperor with the result of their deliberations in the form of an "Imperial assessment" (*Reichsgutachten*). When the emperor gave his approval, the assessment became an "Imperial conclusion" (*Reichsschluss*), which the diet then celebrated solemnly with the emperor (or his proxy), who signed, sealed, and finally published it in print as an "Imperial recess" (*Reichsabschied*).

Unlike in modern institutions, the diet's procedural rules were never written down. As a consequence, they always retained a certain level of flexibility. Although never formally codified, premodern laws nevertheless typically acquired over time a special legal status: that of "praiseworthy precedents" (*löbliches Herkommen*).

Important steps toward the consolidation of the institution of the Imperial diet were the increasing use of written recesses and the growing tendency to close it off to new members. The latter was an especially important development because it determined de facto who enjoyed the status of Imperial immediacy and who did not. The institutionalization of the diet's procedures was fundamental to the integration of Imperial members into a politically functioning unity insofar as the diet's decisions were applicable, at least in theory, to all Imperial members even if they were absent from the diet itself or continued to oppose its resolutions. Older interpretations of the Imperial constitution had seen things differently: only those members who had personally supported a decision were also bound by it (*quod omnes tangit, ab omnibus approbetur* ran the Latin saying: that which concerns all should also be approved by all). In the past, in other words, the very act of absenting oneself from the diet meant that one was not bound by its decisions. Even in the early modern period, many Imperial members did not follow the general obligation to act in accordance with Imperial recesses. Attempts to enforce Imperial recesses on individual estates often failed, especially when the affected estates were particularly powerful. After all, in the Empire there was no executive institution that was independent of such estates. This state of affairs had important consequences in questions of religion, as we shall see later.

Despite all these obstacles, the Imperial diets of the sixteenth century proved quite efficient. They not only served as instruments for raising revenues but also actively shaped Imperial policies. At the beginning of the century, Imperial diets were busy with new legislation: a series of Imperial government regulations (*Reichspoliceyordnungen*) standardized the coin and credit systems, the crafts, and the trades; set common standards for sartorial appearance; and prohibited certain types of luxury. The *Constitutio Criminalis Carolina* of

1532 codified and modernized the form and content of criminal law in the Empire. Such Imperial regulations and laws were secondary: they were relevant only in those areas (geographical or legal) where particular territorial states lacked laws. But even in the territorial states, Imperial law served as a model to be followed. It was influential, in other words, even if not all Imperial members embraced it all the time.

The Imperial diets of the early modern period were different from modern parliaments in important ways. They were the main representative organs of the Empire in the sense that at least in theory they embodied and made visible the entire Empire as a coherent and active body politic. As opposed to modern parliaments, however, the participants in Imperial diets were not elected to their position by anyone, let alone by the subjects in the Empire's individual territories. Their claim to a seat and a vote at the diet was based on the self-assertion of their rulership and authority, either as persons (for example, electors or Imperial princes) or as corporations (such as Imperial cities or abbeys). The whole system was not based on the representation of "the people" or the entire population of the Empire. Sixteenth-century Imperial diets were also still social events of the upper echelons of society, a place where meetings of the heads of the Empire's main noble dynasties took place, often coupled with weddings, enfeoffments, knightly tournaments, hunting expeditions, and so forth; they were as much loci for the meticulous staging of lordship as instruments for solving pressing political problems.

Public peace, the Imperial chamber court, the Common Penny, Imperial diets—the historical significance of the 1495 Imperial diet of Worms did not stop with these four reform laws, especially because some of these reforms did not prove successful in practice. The diet's historical significance also stemmed from the fact that it was in Worms that the Imperial estates for the first time "worked as a coherent body in pursuit of common goals" and that the emperor accepted this in practice (Peter Moraw).

The individual Imperial institutions established in Worms evolved further in the following decades and were even supplemented by new ones, such as the short-lived Imperial governing council (Reichsregiment). The Reichsregiment was an attempt to create a permanent, estates-dominated governmental organ for the whole Empire that would bolster Imperial governmentality in the long run. In form, it resembled the Imperial diet's committees and was led by the Imperial archchancellor, Berthold von Henneberg. It existed for only two years, however, between 1500 and 1502, before falling apart: none of the Imperial estates was willing to surrender its powers permanently to such a body. Emperor Charles V resurrected this defunct body between 1521 and 1530, though this time its purpose was to serve as a replacement for the absent emperor rather than as a representative of the Imperial estates. This is why this second Reichsregiment was headed by the emperor's brother, Roman king and later emperor Ferdinand I. Just like its predecessor, however, the Reichsregiment of 1521–1530 could not assert its authority vis-à-vis the individual Imperial estates. After its failure, no one attempted to resurrect it again.

A much more substantial step toward establishing a permanent set of institutions for the Empire was the creation of the already mentioned Imperial circles. Six such circles were created in 1500 when the Empire was divided into six geographical districts, each encompassing a set of neighboring territories: Franconia, Bavaria, Swabia, the Upper Rhine, the Lower Rhine and Westphalia, and Saxony. At first, the circles served as the basis for the election of members to the Reichsregiment and later to the Imperial chamber court. The 1512 Imperial diet of Cologne established four more circles (the Austrian, Burgundian, Electoral Rhenish, and Upper Saxonian) in order to include the Habsburg possessions and the territories of the Imperial electors in the system. Left out were Italy, the Swiss Confederation, Bohemia, and all Imperial knights. From the 1530s onward, the circles organized their own diets, complete with a head who called them into session (usually the most powerful Imperial member in the circle), a lieutenant, a common treasury, and an archive. The circles developed into versatile executive organs for all those tasks that lay beyond the power of individual Imperial estates but did not affect directly the Empire as a whole—for instance, executing the Imperial courts' verdicts or safeguarding the public peace. Over time the Imperial circles acquired more and more responsibilities, including, most importantly, in the military defense of the Empire against external threats, a role regulated in the Imperial executive orders of 1555 and the Imperial military constitution (Reichskriegsverfassung) of 1682. Other tasks included the regulation of transportation and markets. Not all the circles were active to the same degree. They were most dynamic in those areas where they contained many diverse Imperial estates—for example, in Swabia, Franconia, and the Upper Rhine. They were less effective in those parts of the Empire where one powerful estate dominated all the others—as in Bavaria or Saxony, for instance. The Electoral Rhenish circle was the least active of all, because it included four electors (the archbishops of Mainz, Cologne, and Trier, as well as the count Palatine), and these already cooperated among themselves through the separate meetings of the electors.

The constitution of the circles was typical of the Imperial constitution as a whole. Because of the many deficiencies of the general Imperial executive organs, one had to rely on the cooperation of the affected parties in implementing general decisions. Even in the circles, however, one had little chance to oppose the will of the most powerful estates, which, in turn, often used the circle's institutions only to pursue their own selfish interests. Much in the same way as in the general institutions of the Empire, the circles' institutions worked well only when they succeeded in compensating for the weakness of their middling estates by forming a whole that was stronger than its individual parts.

4

THE CHALLENGE OF THE REFORMATION, 1521–1555

Before they could take root, the new Imperial institutions faced an existential crisis. In 1517, the Augustinian monk Martin Luther published his famous ninety-five theses in the Saxon town of Wittenberg. The reforming movement Luther unleashed in the following years led to conflicts that shook the very foundations of the religious and political order in the Empire. This crisis altered the Imperial institutions, but also, perhaps paradoxically, strengthened them as well.

Charles V, Maximilian I's grandson, was elected Holy Roman Emperor in 1519, thus turning the Habsburgs into perhaps the mightiest dynasty in European history (see p. 46). As a counterweight to this unprecedented concentration of power, the electors dictated to the new emperor an electoral capitulation with the intention of protecting themselves—as well as other Imperial estates—from the looming danger of an overwhelmingly powerful monarch. Nevertheless, the electors could not prevent Charles from pursuing his dynastic great-power politics in the Empire, a move he legitimized, at least in part, by highlighting the old idea of the universality of his office. The new emperor was especially convinced of his responsibility to sustain and reform the *one* Church. At least at first, many humanists and reformers hoped that he would step up and assume exactly this role. Indeed, in his famous *Address to the Christian Nobility of the German Nation* (1520), Luther himself urged the young emperor and other German princes to follow through on the ubiquitous calls for the reform of the Church. Such calls were not new and were based in part on the late medieval and early modern "grievances of the German nation" (*gravamina nationis Germanicae*): long catalogs of complaints about real or purported abuses of the German nation by the papal curia. The pope had innumerable prerogatives in the German territories that allowed him to extract large sums of money from their inhabitants. His rights to allocate benefices, sell indulgences, and dispense with canon law gave him recourse to huge financial resources. Over time these resources helped the pope turn the patrimonial possessions of the Catholic Church into a veritable early modern state, complete with a luxurious court, a modern military, a substantial network of political clients, and solid financial administration.

With his fundamental critique of indulgences, Luther struck the innermost chord of the grievances. His aim was not a political one; he was concerned with the salvation of Christian souls, not with governing states. But Luther's radically simple message about the need for reforming the Church had unintended political consequences. If, as Luther claimed, man could reach salvation through his faith, divine grace, and Holy Scripture alone, there was no need for all the mediating institutions between him and God; the Church, politically speaking, was superfluous. Especially consequential for the future of the Empire's constitution was Luther's teachings about the need to distinguish between the religious and secular orders in the world, between the internal life and the social life of man, and between the court of conscience and the court of rulers. The implication of these teachings was that the Church—both the pope himself and all Imperial prelates—should possess no political power. But the Imperial constitution, as we saw, resembled a rich fabric woven of both religious and secular threads. If Luther's doctrines were to prevail, who would take over the rights and functions of the Imperial church?

As is well known, Luther's ideas found extremely rich soil in both urban and rural communities across Germany and spread far and wide through sermons, pamphlets, and broadsides. Their impact on the Empire, however, was not predetermined. In early 1521, the pope excommunicated Luther and declared him a heretic. The pope waited now for the Empire to also officially outlaw the would-be reformer, but many Imperial estates hesitated. As they read it, Luther's *Address to the Christian Nobility* was an extremely welcome call for a national religious renewal. The "Luther question," they consequently decided, was a national issue that Charles V should discuss with them in his first Imperial diet, scheduled to meet in Worms in 1521. The religious question would by no means be the most important issue on the agenda of this diet. Superseding it was the need to reestablish the Reichsregiment and the drawing up of a new tax register for the Empire.

Charles V was willing to declare Luther an outlaw right away, not least because he needed papal support in his conflict with France. But a majority among the Imperial estates who attended the diet objected to such high-handed treatment of Luther by the emperor and managed to push through a judicial hearing for the Saxon monk. This was the background of Luther's appearance in front of the emperor, his retinue, and the Imperial princes on April 17–18, 1521, in which he famously refused to recant.

All attempts at reconciliation and mediation ultimately failed. After Luther's hearing, Charles V outlawed him with an edict he composed in his own hand, basing his decision to oppose the Imperial estates on his duty as emperor to protect the Roman Church and the Catholic faith. This argument went along the traditional lines of Imperial politics: that which one's predecessors had maintained and protected for so many centuries could not be tossed aside arbitrarily.

It was therefore also the duty of the Imperial estates, Charles maintained, to cooperate with him against the notorious heretic Martin Luther. On April 30, 1521, the Imperial estates still present at Worms (many had left in the meantime) finally agreed to support the emperor and outlaw Luther. In the Edict of Worms (May 8, 1521), Charles forbade all Imperial estates from maintaining contact with Luther, reading his books, or helping him spread his ideas. Those unwilling to follow the edict would become outlaws themselves. Apart from being excommunicated from the body of Christ (the Church), Luther was now also a reject of the body politic (the Empire). This legal status defined Luther for the rest of his life and considerably restricted his movement; his ideas, however, suffered no such fate.

During the 1520s, it became clear that the emperor could not force the Edict of Worms on the Luther-friendly estates. From 1521 to 1530, the emperor wasn't even in Germany. Leaving the administration of the Empire to his brother Ferdinand and the newly created Reichsregiment, he spent his time pursuing Habsburg interests by fighting against King Francis I of France and, from 1526 to 1529, also against the pope. The latter he first defeated in battle; then, in Bologna in 1530, he made the pope crown him (Charles) as emperor. In the meantime, the Imperial estates never stopped urging Charles to summon a national council of the church in Germany to discuss the question of reform; they wanted, in other words, to take a lead in handling the religious question in the Empire. Charles rejected this idea, held out a promise for a future general council of the Church, and meanwhile tried to enforce the Edict of Worms from afar. Gradually, the battle lines were drawn: the Habsburgs, the dukes of Bavaria, Duke George of Saxony, Elector Joachim of Brandenburg, and the ecclesiastical princes were facing several princes who were clearly leaning toward Luther's movement or were still considering their options, such as Landgrave Philip of Hesse, Albert of Brandenburg (head of the Teutonic Knights), and the elector of Saxony.

These front lines often cut through the great princely dynasties. Already by the mid-1520s, one could detect the nascent lines of future confessionally oriented political alliances in the Empire. These lines would characterize German politics throughout the sixteenth and early seventeenth centuries, until the end of the Thirty Years' War in 1648.

The Imperial diet of Speyer in 1526 witnessed an important development. In exchange for their willingness to pay Imperial taxes, the estates suggested that the emperor accept a compromise: each estate would be responsible for the enforcement of the Edict of Worms in its own territories in such a way that it could justify its conduct "before God and the emperor." Since it proved impossible to reach a general consensus on the religious question, the estates agreed to follow the Edict of Worms de jure by de facto implementing it in their own territories as they saw fit. This solution corresponded to pre-Reformation tendencies to establish territorial control over religious questions and laid the foundations for the estates' future right to church reform (ius reformandi). Ferdinand, in Charles's absence, had no choice but to accept this solution because he relied on the Imperial estates to raise funds for his brother's military campaigns and because the implementation of the Edict of Worms was impossible without the cooperation of the Imperial estates. The temporary compromise created a general model for any future negotiated solution.

Three years later, with Emperor Charles still absent and his brother Ferdinand taking his place as stadtholder, the Imperial diet met once more. The place was again the city of Speyer, and the formal occasion, also once again, was the Ottoman threat to the Empire's southeastern provinces. Unlike the diet of 1526, however, the new diet took place in an especially hostile atmosphere—shortly beforehand, Landgrave Philip of Hesse attacked Mainz and Würzburg to preempt a supposed anti-Lutheran conspiracy. Ferdinand's plan was to force the Imperial estates to put a final and definitive stop to the spread of the Reformation in the Empire. In the diet itself, a majority made up of Catholic estates supported Ferdinand's proposition, while the other estates present, leaning toward the reformed doctrines, filed a formal "protestation" against it. They included Elector John of Saxony, Landgrave Philip of Hesse, Margrave George of Brandenburg-Ansbach, Duke Ernst of Braunschweig-Lüneburg, Prince Wolfgang of Anhalt, and fourteen Imperial cities, including the important urban centers of Strasbourg, Nuremberg, and Ulm. Such a protestation (the source of the later term "Protestants") was common in the Holy Roman Empire. It was a legal move by which an Imperial estate or member challenged the binding character of a given Imperial policy or resolution. In this case, the minority party claimed that questions of conscience could not be arbitrated on the Imperial level through a simple majority vote. By raising such an objection, they questioned more generally the diet's ability to make binding decisions. Because the diet's recess included the majority opinion despite the objections, the protesting estates appealed to the emperor, who was then campaigning in northern Italy. This appeal, too, proved futile.

In 1530, after a hiatus of almost a decade, Emperor Charles V finally returned to Germany. He came in person to the Imperial diet of Augsburg, showing willingness to listen to the differing theological arguments. On very short notice, the Lutheran theologians, led by Philip Melanchthon, formulated their position, the famous Augsburg Confession (*Confessio Augustana*), which they then presented to the emperor. The Augsburg Confession played an important role in the following years because it provided a series of definitions that would later help form the legal basis for the religious compromise in the Empire. Simultaneously, four southern German cities formulated their own confession of faith—the so-called *Confessio Tetrapolitana* ("Confession of the Four Cities")—and Ulrich Zwingli added his own *Ratio fidei* ("Ground of Faith"). Charles V dismissed Zwingli's tractate but commissioned from the Catholic side a refutation

(*Confutatio*) of the Augsburg Confession. Despite attempts from both sides to find common theological ground, all attempts at definitive compromise eventually failed. Thus, a majority in the diet supported Charles V's proposed taxes while also reaffirming the Edict of Worms. In response, numerous Protestant princes and cities formed the Smalkaldic League in 1531. This alliance in defense of "God's Word in the world," as they put it, was a legitimate tool of resistance against an emperor who would not follow his own elective capitulations. Later, Luther gave his blessing to this position.

In the meantime, the social and political consequences of the Reformation became all the more visible. The 1520s were a tumultuous time in many urban and rural communities in Germany. Works of individual reforming preachers spread far and wide through new forms of mass media, making Germany awash with anticlerical riots and violent actions against the Catholic Mass, religious images, and other devotional objects. Priests began to marry, and monks and nuns left their abbeys. The demands were similar in many places: pure teachings of the Gospel, free communal election of priests, the administration of the Eucharist in both kinds, and the control of communal ecclesiastical property by the community itself. As the reform movement became more diverse, it also began to move in different directions, forming quite distinct social, economic, and political alliances along the way. In 1522, for instance, several Imperial knights formed an alliance under the leadership of Franz von Sickingen, who led them against their common neighbor, the elector of Mainz, in the name of the Gospel. The fusion of reforming and general economic and social demands led in 1524–1525 to a "Peasants' War." Participants in this series of revolts across Germany justified their actions by invoking Scripture, a tactic that gave their fight more coherence, conceptually and politically, than earlier such incidents. The rebelling peasants formed supra-regional alliances, created general organizational structures, and at times even won over burghers to their cause. The emperor and many of the Empire's princes took to arms and beat the peasants decisively. Assisting them in their efforts was Martin Luther himself, who opposed the peasants' action with passion, as well as the Swabian League, a military association of widely diverse Imperial estates formed in 1488 under Habsburg leadership. In many urban communities—especially in Imperial cities—demands for religious reform were coupled with guild demands for more political participation vis-à-vis city oligarchies. At the time, it seemed as if the reform movement was above all a matter of the Common Man.

Nevertheless, already in the 1520s some figures of authority began to lean toward the Reformation. In the majority of the Imperial cities as well as in many other urban centers, communal authorities often embraced the Reformation either peacefully or after overcoming open conflict. The Reformation, after all, advanced communal autonomy (for example, through the free election of priests), a fact that local elites did not fail to recognize. Taking Zwingli's work in Zurich as their principal model, these authorities introduced the preaching of the "pure Gospel," did away with the Catholic Mass, shut down abbeys, confiscated church property, abolished the privileges of the priesthood, took the caring of the poor and the management of schools into their own hands, and issued a series of new church ordinances and marriage and moral codes.

Already in the 1520s, several territorial lords had introduced the Reformation in their own lands. They did so for the same reasons as the urban elites. The prime example in this respect was the head of the order of the Teutonic Knights, Albert of Brandenburg, in his Prussian territories. Several princes recognized early on how advantageous it would be for them to expand their own power at the expense of the Church by closing down abbeys, mediatizing and secularizing bishoprics, and taking over formerly ecclesiastical privileges and immunities. Territorial lords explained such extreme measures by claiming the position of "emergency bishops"—someone, they claimed, had to fill the vacuum left by the dissolution of the Roman

Church in their lands. All of this led to the creation of instruments of control and organization—central church administration, religious regulations, regular visitations, and so forth—that allowed territorial lords to intervene in the lives of their subjects like never before (pp. 77–78).

Contradictions and conflicts within the reform movement were present almost from its inception. Most important in this respect were the differences between Lutherans, on the one hand, and the southern, Zwinglian reformers, on the other hand. Most Imperial cities leaned toward Zwingli's doctrines, which differed from Luther's with respect to the question of the Eucharist and various ecclesiological matters. Despite their internal divisions, however, the upper echelons of society, whether urban or landed, Catholic or Protestant, shared a fundamental aim: the need to fight against the radical, spiritualist, anabaptist movement within the Reformation, which anticipated an immediate Second Coming and either called for a complete withdrawal from the worldly order or sought to hasten the arrival of the End of Days. In 1529, the Imperial diet prescribed the death penalty for all members of such radical groups.

Even during the tumultuous 1530s and 1540s, the Imperial diet never stopped discussing common political matters. The Protestant estates continued to support the Empire financially, and the diet continued to discuss Imperial recesses and to promulgate new Imperial laws. As long as Charles V continued to be tied down abroad by his conflicts with France and the Ottomans, he had to postpone a definitive solution to the religious question in the Empire. The Imperial chamber court kept pushing back its resolution in the legal proceedings against the Protestant estates, and the Imperial estates repeatedly suspended the implementation of the Edict of Worms—for example, in the Religious Peace of Nuremberg in 1532, or the Religious Peace of Frankfurt seven years later. Such developments notwithstanding, many in the Empire still hoped to reach a formula that would settle the religious schism once and for all, and discussions between Catholic and Protestant theologians never completely subsided. All of this, it turned out, was to no avail.

The summer of 1546 saw a radical transformation of the political-religious situation. Freed from his engagements abroad, Charles V finally turned his attention back to Germany. His goal was to solve the religious question in the Empire definitively and, if necessary, by force. As justification for his military actions against the Protestants in the Smalkaldic War (1546–1547), Charles invoked the Imperial ban on the two leaders of the Smalkaldic League, Philip of Hesse and John Frederick of Saxony. Charles was the undisputed winner in the ensuing military conflict—not least because Duke Maurice of Saxony switched sides in the middle of the war, an action for which Charles repaid him by transferring the office of elector of Saxony from Maurice's uncle (John Frederick) to Maurice himself. During the war, Charles reached the zenith of his power. He beat the Smalkaldic League militarily, captured both of its leaders, had all the defeated Protestant princes and cities submit to him in an elaborate ceremony of genuflection, and even forced the southern German cities (whose guilds he held responsible for igniting the conflict) to adopt patrician constitutions.

In 1548, during the Imperial diet of Augsburg, Charles tried to cash in on his successes of the previous year. His aim was twofold: to incorporate the Protestants once again into the Old Church (while also acknowledging that the latter had to undergo some reforms), and to break the power and liberties of the Imperial estates by establishing a stronger, centralized Imperial authority over the whole Empire, dominated by him.

Charles sought to reach the first of these goals through the Augsburg Interim (from the Latin *interim*, "in the meantime"). This was a general framework for a temporary solution to the religious schism in the Empire, under the auspices of the emperor, until a more permanent solution could be reached through a general council of the Church. (Such a council had already started its work in the northern

Italian city of Trent in 1545.) The Interim compelled the Protestants to return in principle to the old faith and its religious practices, and it demanded that they return all confiscated church property to its rightful owner. In return, the Interim allowed priests to marry and the communion chalice to be shared with the laity. Although the Interim was passed into law by a Catholic majority, it applied only to the Protestant estates. Constitutionally, it signified an unprecedented claim by the emperor to rule over questions of faith across the Empire—a claim that went above and beyond his older, medieval role as defender of Christendom.

The emperor attempted to accomplish the second of his aims in the Imperial diet of 1548 through an agenda of political-constitutional renewal. He planned a novel form of association between the emperor and individual Imperial estates that, had it materialized, would have undermined the Imperial diet and deprived it of its main political functions. Members of the new association were to help maintain a permanent army under the emperor's command and to pay him a permanent tax. The new diet would have differed markedly from the old one, replacing its tricameral structure with a unified assembly that would also include the Imperial knights and perhaps even other, non-immediate nobles in the territorial states, all with their equal vote in the diet's proceedings, regardless of social rank. Such a diet would have fundamentally shifted the power relations within the Empire; the electors, for instance, would have seen their seven votes submerged by a sea of hundreds of others. The emperor would have occupied the pinnacle of a largely leveled-out Imperial association and could have used the diet, as never before, as an instrument for the execution of his policies. This attempt at an almost revolutionary overhaul of the diet failed exactly because of the opposition of those who stood to lose the most from it—especially, of course, the electors. They managed to frustrate Charles's attempts in this direction and eventually to grind them to a halt. Even the implementation of the Interim proved difficult: early attempts to enforce it—in the duchy of Württemberg, for instance—made very little progress. It became clear that one could not roll back the confessional divisions of the preceding decades. The liberties of the Imperial princes and their net political weight as the lords in their own territories simply posed too powerful an obstacle to Charles's plans. More and more people began to realize that the confessional divisions in the Empire were there to stay. The emperor could not overcome them by force. He had to deal with them through a modified framework of the Imperial constitution.

The Princes' War of 1552 caused a sudden change in the political situation. Maurice of Saxony changed sides once again, forming an alliance with other Protestant opponents of the emperor as well as with the king of France. (The French king, incidentally, persecuted Protestants in his own lands quite brutally). In exchange for the French king's assistance in the revolt, Maurice and his German allies promised him the Imperial bishoprics of Metz, Toul, and Verdun. Charles V found himself in a weak position and had to withdraw to his territories in the Low Countries. Ferdinand, Charles's brother, came to a temporary understanding with the rebelling princes in the Peace of Passau (1552), a compromise that Charles opposed but that nonetheless set the terms for the Religious Peace of Augsburg in 1555. In the Second Margrave War of 1552–1554, Charles's support for a notorious breaker of the public peace only helped undermine his own legitimacy as a broker of a just solution to the religious conflict. In 1556, Charles finally withdrew to a monastery in Spain and abdicated the Imperial throne.

Three decades after the beginning of the Reformation, it became clear that the religious schism and its political consequences were not going away anytime soon. Military force, theological debates and negotiations, a general Church council, legal actions by the Imperial chamber court—nothing could turn back the clock on the developments of the preceding decades. In 1555, the Imperial diet of Augsburg finally drew the logical conclusion from this situation and reached an epoch-making compromise. The negotiations during the diet took place between Ferdinand as the emperor's representative (but without his consent) and the Imperial estates. The two sides reached an agreement because they left aside the question of their respective theological truth claims and concentrated instead on finding a legal framework through which the differing confessions would coexist without undermining the entire Imperial constitution.

The most important element of the deal of 1555 was a peace treaty between the two confessions: the Catholic Imperial estates, on the one side, and those estates that adhered to the Augsburg Confession of 1530, on the other side. The Religious Peace of Augsburg prohibited all estates from oppressing, suppressing, or forcefully coercing any other Imperial estate (or its subjects) in all religious questions. It went even further and legalized retrospectively some earlier attacks on Imperial and canon laws. Thus, the secularization of Church property by Protestant princes and cities became law as long as these actions had taken place before 1552 (that is, before the Peace of Passau). Finally, the peace suspended the Church's jurisdiction over Protestants, although the pope, for his part, continued to view Protestants as subject to canon law and thus also as heretics.

To guarantee its implementation on the ground, the peace of 1555 was followed by a series of concrete measures. The Imperial chamber court underwent important reforms and included Protestant assessors after 1555. A new executive order entrusted the handling of the peace to the Imperial circles and established a whole hierarchy of authorities to sanction breakers of the peace, starting with the lords in whose territories the breach occurred, continuing with the relevant Imperial circle(s), and ending at the top with a general diet of Imperial deputies (*Reichsdeputationstag*)—a kind of committee of the entire Imperial diet but without the emperor. The diet intervened only if this entire legal hierarchy proved unsuccessful. Through these measures, the peace of 1555 hollowed out to a large extent the emperor's traditional role as the prime defender of peace as well as his right to use force unilaterally against particular Imperial estates.

The second fundamental measure in the Religious Peace of 1555 gave the territorial lords the right to establish an official confession in their own lands. This was the famous ius reformandi ("right of reformation"), which jurists would later sum up in the formula *cuius regio eius religio*: "whose realm, his religion." Territorial lords could now make up their own minds about the theological claims of the opposing confessions, and they could also force their subjects to follow their decision. In an important sense, the peace of 1555 reaffirmed the old constitutional principle that the Imperial legal framework applied only to the Imperial estates and not to their subjects. The latter were excluded from the very same religious toleration that the different estates swore to practice between themselves. Nevertheless, one can find in the Peace of Augsburg early signs of a more general or abstract conception of religious toleration, including even for territorial subjects. Thus, if a ruler's subjects professed a faith different from his own, he could not prevent them from leaving his lands. Moreover, the peace recognized and guaranteed the biconfessional status of those Imperial cities that contained both Protestant and Catholic populations, largely in order to protect Catholics living in the predominantly Protestant Imperial cities. With the Interim, the emperor began to change this state of affairs by reintroducing Catholicism into the cities. The Peace of Augsburg wrote this now into law and protected Catholics in otherwise Protestant urban communities.

The peace reached in Augsburg was possible only because all sides were exhausted from the never-ending religious conflict. Recognizing that a series of problems remained unsolved, they sought a formula—however temporary—that would camouflage the problems rather than solve them once and for all. The built-in disagreements, ambiguities, and contradictions in the peace would resurface soon enough. This was especially true for the *reservatum ecclesiasticum* ("ecclesiastical reservation"), which formed an important exception to the principle of the ius reformandi in the Empire's individual territories. According to this regulation, if an ecclesiastical prince left the Catholic faith, he would lose his office, lands, and property, and a Catholic prince would be elected to succeed him. The ecclesiastical princes were consequently not granted their ius reformandi, a measure taken to prevent the formation of a Protestant majority in the chamber of electors or other Imperial bodies. Ferdinand introduced this regulation personally into the peace, and the Protestant estates rejected it at first out of hand. They eventually tolerated its inclusion in the Imperial recess of 1555 in exchange for Ferdinand's concession (which, however, he issued as a separate document, that is, not as part of the recess of 1555) that the territorial nobility and cities located within ecclesiastical principalities could stick to the Protestant confession if they wished to do so. The question of how this so-called Ferdinandine Declaration (*Declaratio Ferdinandea*) could be enforced remained open.

A major contradiction in the Peace of Augsburg was that, although it granted territorial lords the ius reformandi over their lands, it legalized only secularizations of church property that had taken place before the Peace of Passau in 1552. It consequently remained unclear how a ruler could further (legally) secularize church property, if at all. The legal situation in the Imperial cities was also ambiguous, because it remained uncertain whether city councils enjoyed the same rights as territorial princes and also whether they possessed the ius reformandi or not. Another unresolved issue was the question of who belonged legally to the Augsburg Confession and who did not, as well as who might be able to answer such a question in the first place. This was a crucial issue, because the Peace of Augsburg guaranteed religious freedom only to adherents of the Augsburg Confession and not, for instance, to Calvinists, who rejected this formula. Finally, the Peace of Augsburg contained conflicting statements regarding its own status, especially in relation to the question of whether it was meant to be a permanent Imperial law or only a temporary solution before a definitive settlement could be reached. The two sides in the diet viewed the matter quite differently. The Protestants saw in the peace of 1555 a general, final, and constitutionally unalterable Imperial law that placed the two confessions in the Empire on equal footing. The Catholics, for their part, viewed the peace as an exception to the otherwise still-prevailing rights of the Church—a temporary compromise they had the right to rescind in the future, should different circumstances arise.

The Religious Peace of Augsburg was a major milestone in the constitutional history of the Holy Roman Empire. It did not settle the confessional problems once and for all, but it did prevent the religious splintering *in* the Empire from becoming a political disintegration *of* the Empire. It legalized and formalized confessional cohabitation by leaving the theological issues unresolved. All of this signified a stark departure from the medieval perception of the Empire as a divinely ordained body whose harmonious and eternal unity was possible only by its reliance on both worldly and ecclesiastical law—the legitimacy of human laws rested on their agreement with divine decrees. From a Catholic perspective, Imperial law now protected outright heretics who actively sought to undermine divine law. Because it compelled two competing conceptions of religious truth to coexist within the same political body, the Peace of Augsburg helped distinguish between religion and politics—a development of great and at first only poorly understood consequences that nonetheless were relevant at first only at the level of the Imperial estates. At the level of the individual territorial states, on the other hand, the consequences of the peace of 1555 were the exact opposite: for the first time, territorial princes could unify religious and political authority in their own hands.

5

FROM THE CONSOLIDATION TO THE CRISIS OF THE IMPERIAL INSTITUTIONS, 1555–1618

Generally speaking, the period after 1555 was one of peaceful co-existence between the different confessions in the Empire. Because the policies of Emperors Ferdinand I (1558–1564) and Maximilian II (1564–1576) were conciliatory and consensus-oriented in nature (Maximilian even sympathized with the Protestants), the Imperial institutions functioned better in this period than either before or after. The electors especially—with the exception of the count Palatine—cooperated closely with each other and with the emperor, regardless of their specific confessional affiliations. The Turkish threat played an important role in all of this: after 1547, the Habsburgs paid out high contributions to the Ottoman sultan, and although they frequently signed formal ceasefire agreements with him, latent fears about the Turks were never far from the surface. A steady stream of pamphlets and broadsides kept alive anxieties about the "Archenemy of Christendom" and helped motivate the Imperial estates both to vote for and to actually pay high taxes to the emperor. Only in 1606, with the conclusion of the Peace of Zsitva-torok between the Habsburgs and the Ottomans, did the Imperial estates' motivation to cooperate with each other across confessional lines began to subside.

The Empire successfully combated local breaches of the public peace. In the 1560s, for instance, the knight Wilhelm von Grumbach, backed by Duke John Frederick II of Saxony, pursued a blood feud that threatened to expand and include other members of the lower nobility. The affected Imperial circles, relying on the procedures established in the Religious Peace of Augsburg, fought against Grumbach both at court and on the battlefield, eventually defeating and executing him. At the same time, the limits of the Empire's military efficiency also became clear. In 1570, the Habsburg general Lazarus von Schwendi laid a plan before the Imperial diet for the creation of a standing Imperial army under the emperor's supreme command. His idea was to give the Empire sufficient means to pursue an expansive power politics in Europe. The Imperial estates quickly closed their ranks and opposed von Schwendi's plan, which ultimately failed. The territorial lords, especially but not only the Protestant ones, supported the Imperial constitution only as long as it helped them consolidate power in their own lands.

Under the aegis of the Religious Peace of Augsburg, the confessionalization of the Empire's individual territories proceeded at a steady pace. In the course of the sixteenth century, the religious schism brought about a situation in which three distinct confessional churches coexisted in the Empire, each defined by its own confessional creed: Lutheranism, with its Augsburg Confession of 1530 and the Formula of Concord of 1577; the Reformed (Calvinist) confession, with the Heidelberg Catechism of 1563 serving as a model for individual territorial churches; and for the Catholic Church, the 1563 creed of Pope Pius IV (*Professio fidei Tridentina*). In the Council of Trent (1545–1563), the Catholic Church finally embraced parts of the reformist agenda that it had previously opposed. Nevertheless, the hopes of Charles V and some of the

Imperial estates that the council would help heal the religious schism in the Empire proved vain; all indications pointed to an attempt by the council to condemn the Lutheran "heresy" and hold it in check rather than find common ground with it. The Old Church faced the challenge of Protestantism by redefining and reasserting its own doctrines and by modernizing its institutions. Although its theology was certainly different from that of Luther's followers, the Catholic Church caught up with many of the specific political practices that Protestant princes had been implementing in their territories. To accomplish this, the post-Tridentine Church relied especially heavily on newly created religious orders, first and foremost among them the Society of Jesus (the Jesuits).

The gradual formation of clear confessional boundaries in the Empire gave further impetus to processes of state-building in individual territories and to parallel modernization efforts in both the Catholic and Protestant camps. The religious schism gave individual princes an opportunity to take control over religious questions. This was true for the Protestant princes as well as, under certain restrictions, the Catholic ones. By enforcing and controlling religious doctrines and practices in their individual territories, princes of the three confessions expanded their authority and power (at least in theory) over all their subjects without exception. More than ever before, princes sought to control and regulate their subjects' faith and day-to-day behavior. They did so by integrating the church into state administration; releasing a flood of official regulations about ecclesiastical affairs, moral conduct, marriage and family matters, and public order; conducting thorough visitations of all their parishes; establishing schools and universities for the education of confessionally reliable jurists and theologians; and much more. Authorities in the Empire's cities and territories successfully legitimized such actions by claiming that they had responsibility to care for the souls of their subjects and that they were acting for the glorification of God's name.

As long as the confessional stalemate in the Empire persisted, the different sides sought to manage (rather than settle definitively) their precarious coexistence. But as soon as one side became more powerful politically and started entertaining ideas of strengthening its position at the other sides' expense, the Religious Peace of Augsburg began to totter. In the last third of the sixteenth century, the confessional balance of power began to tip in favor of the Catholics. In the wake of the Council of Trent, the Protestants had to give up any hope of reunifying the Church under their banner. The decades-long triumphal march of Protestantism across the Empire ground to a halt, and in the 1570s even receded. Two factors contributed to this new situation. First, many Catholic princes whose subjects and territorial estates had embraced Lutheranism earlier in the century began a sustained campaign to re-Catholicize them, putting Lutherans on the defensive. Worse still was the fact that the internal antagonisms among the Protestants became ever more pronounced. Ever since the 1560s, an increasing number of Imperial estates had followed the example of the count Palatine and converted to Calvinism, a branch of Protestantism that sought to go beyond Luther's call for a "reform of doctrine" and embrace also a "reform of life"—that is, a general discipline of manners, from regularly attending church services on Sundays to keeping a godly Christian household. (Historians usually refer to this as the "Second Reformation.") Often, the theological disputes between Lutherans and Calvinists were far more heated than their respective disagreements with Catholics. This is why attempts to find a middle ground between the two Protestant confessions ended in failure (for example, in Brandenburg and in the principality of Jülich-Cleves). All indications pointed toward increasing splintering in the Protestant camp in the future.

From the start, the consensus of 1555 stood on shaky ground. As we saw, it was based on a series of ad-hoc concessions and consisted of textual formulations that were open to widely different interpretations. Ever since the 1560s—and contrary to the *Declaratio*

Ferdinandea—a long list of Catholic rulers pursued aggressive re-Catholicization policies vis-à-vis their predominantly Lutheran estates. This was the case, among many other places, in Bavaria, Fulda, Würzburg, and in certain parts of the Habsburg lands, such as Inner Austria and the Tyrol. For their part, Protestant rulers infringed from the start on those provisions in the Peace of Augsburg that were intended to prevent the secularization of the ecclesiastical principalities. Especially in northern Germany, which geographically and politically had always lain farthest from the Empire's control, princes and cities secularized almost all bishoprics. At first, they appointed special "administrators" (usually the sons of the territorial lords) to run the bishoprics, then they annexed them formally to their lands. As in the past, they also continued to seize non-immediate church property located in their territories. Several Protestant princes—most importantly, the Palatine elector—disputed in the Imperial diets of the 1560s and 1570s the provisions that restricted their ius reformandi. The issue for this group of princes—who formed what in German is known as the Freistellungsbewegung (the "exemption movement")—was the question not only of the confessional affiliation of prince-bishops and prelates but also of canons of collegiate churches and cathedral chapters. The Religious Peace of Augsburg was ambiguous regarding the question of whether such canons lost their offices and sinecures if they converted to Protestantism. This was a matter of great consequence for the lower Protestant nobility, from which many of these canons came. Whereas the Protestants interpreted the ecclesiastical provision of the Peace of Augsburg in a restricted sense, the Catholics sought to expand it, claiming that the provision applied not only to bishoprics but also to all other church benefices, even if these lay within a territorial state. According to this interpretation, if a territorial lord converted to Protestantism, he immediately lost these properties, and if canons converted, they immediately lost their offices and sinecures.

In the years immediately after 1555, Imperial institutions still addressed or channeled such conflicts successfully, but the situation began to change in the 1580s, during the reign of Emperor Rudolf II. The slow departure from the scene of an older generation of moderate princes, such as August of Saxony, contributed first to the escalation of long-standing confessional disputes, then to the eruption of a series of spectacularly violent conflicts. Imperial diets, which traditionally served as arenas of mediation, did not take place for more than a decade (1582–1594). At the same time, the confessional dispute within the Empire was increasingly intertwined with other European conflicts. Both the Catholic and Protestant sides in the Empire had foreign allies: the Protestants were supported by the similarly minded forces in the rebelling Low Countries and in Geneva, while the Catholics had Spain and the pope at their back. Because of the confessional wars in the Low Countries and France, Protestants felt threatened across Europe. As confessional solidarity among both Catholics and Protestant built up, transconfessional forms of solidarity among the estates and in the Empire as a whole became weaker; eventually, they would disappear altogether.

An important catalyst in the escalation of confessional tensions was the 1582 decision by the archbishop-elector of Cologne, Gebhard Truchsess von Waldburg, to convert to Calvinism and secularize his archdiocese. Had Waldburg not been defeated militarily in 1589, his decision could have led to a Protestant majority in the chamber of electors and posed a direct threat to the Habsburg traditional monopoly over the emperor's office. Tied to this so-called Cologne War was the conflict over the cathedral chapter in Strasbourg, a city that in the sixteenth century still lay within the Empire's boundaries. (It would be annexed to France in the late seventeenth century.) The cathedral chapter in Strasbourg was composed of members of the Imperial high nobility, and it had already been dominated by a Protestant majority before the 1580s. In 1583, the pope took away the benefices of four of the chapter's Protestant canons, including that of the archbishop-elector of Cologne (the above-mentioned Gebhard Truchsess von Waldburg). The Protestant city council supported the four canons with military force. The chapter split, and when the local bishop's see became vacant in 1591, each of the two sides elected its own new bishop. Both bishops came from powerful dynasties: on the one hand, the House of Lorraine (which was related to the Habsburgs through multiple family ties) and the Brandenburg Hohenzollerns, on the other hand. These dynastic connections raised the political stakes in this otherwise local conflict and drew in even the emperor himself. In 1604, the Protestant claimant was forced to resign, so the Strasbourg diocese eventually remained Catholic. In the following years, the emperor, with the pope's backing, made sure to fill the northern German bishoprics of Lüttich, Münster, Paderborn, Osnabrück, and Hildesheim with Catholic candidates, often from the Bavarian branch of the Wittelsbach dynasty. The pope also had a permanent nuncio in Cologne from then on. In this way, the Catholics maintained their majority in the Imperial diet.

Although in theory the Peace of Augsburg guaranteed religious coexistence in the Imperial cities, conflicts on the ground were in fact quite common. Especially in the Empire's cities, religion was anything but a strictly personal issue: it influenced social life in almost every conceivable respect. A glaring example was the conflict in 1582 surrounding the calendar reform of Pope Gregory XIII. Despite the fact that astronomers on both sides of the confessional divide supported such a reform, Protestants dubbed it a "Popish concoction" and rejected it as a threat to the salvation of their souls. As a result, the two main confessions in the Empire used two different dating systems until the end of the seventeenth century. In biconfessional Augsburg, the question of calendar reform even led to open conflict and violent riots. The main issue here was whether authorities in Imperial cities had the same ius reformandi as authorities in other Imperial estates. In Aachen, a conflict over the same question almost spun out of control. When the city council affirmed its ius reformandi, it unleashed a heated dispute with the Catholic estates in the Imperial diet. In 1598, after the city council refused to accept the verdict of the Imperial Aulic council against it, the emperor outlawed the entire city council and reinstated the confessional status quo of 1555. The result was a complete re-Catholicization of the city council. Even more extreme was the case of the Imperial city of Donauwörth, in Swabia. Here, the Peace of Augsburg guaranteed confessional parity despite a clear Protestant majority in the population. In 1606, the Protestants barred the Catholics from holding a religious procession through the city streets and a riot broke out. The bishop of Augsburg filed a complaint against Donauwörth with the Imperial Aulic council, which in 1607 placed the entire city under Imperial ban. Instead of entrusting the execution of the ban to the rulers of the Swabian circle (as was common practice), the emperor appointed Duke Maximilian of Bavaria to execute it. Despite vehement protests by the circle's members, Maximilian went beyond the original spirit of the emperor's orders. He occupied the city, forced the population at sword point to reinstate Catholic practices, and eventually robbed Donauwörth of its Imperial immediate status and annexed it to his domains.

The Religious Peace of Augsburg proved especially self-contradictory and conflict-laden when it came to questions about the secularization or mediatization of church property. The peace recognized such practices only if they had taken place before 1552, but territorial princes intent on them after 1555 could also evoke their ius reformandi, which the peace also affirmed. By the late sixteenth century, several lawsuits against post-1555 secularizations were pending at the Imperial chamber court, and in the 1590s the court decided against the Protestant side in four such cases (the so-called four abbeys dispute). Even though the Imperial chamber court also included Protestant assessors, the court's decision gave many Protestants the impression that it increasingly settled questions about church property against them. This contributed to the Protestants' growing sense of isolation and danger.

Taken together, the conflicts and disputes of the half-century after 1555 gradually contributed to the paralysis of the Imperial institutions. To function at all, the Empire relied on consensus among its estates with regard to procedural questions and on the estates' willingness to submit to common decisions. As long as such decisions were the result of compromise and political common ground across confessional lines, the Empire's institutions worked relatively well. But when one side gained a structural advantage over the other, the whole system lost its balance. This is exactly what happened when the Catholic majority among the Imperial estates began to rely on the majority principle in the Imperial diet rather than on the older tradition—vehemently defended by the Protestants—of compromise and consensual decisions. Because the Protestants were a minority in all the Empire's institutions (including the Imperial diet), they ended up always drawing the short straw. Thus, the confessional polarization in the Empire gradually stultified its institutions.

The battle lines were already clearly drawn in the Imperial diet of 1594, which was originally convened in response to the outbreak of yet another war with the Ottomans. Still, the urgency of the military situation in the southeast caused the two sides to reach a precarious agreement, at least with respect to raising funds for the war effort. In the Imperial diet of 1597–1598, however, the situation began to escalate. Led by the Palatine elector, the Protestant estates rejected for the first time the majority principle in voting taxes for the war against the Ottomans. The Imperial chamber court got involved and ruled against the Protestants, who had to give in for the time being. Simultaneously, the work of the Imperial chamber court itself became a bone of contention. Controlling and reviewing the court was the role of an annual visitation committee composed of a rotating number of Imperial estates. By the time of the Imperial diets of the

1590s, the visitation committee had stopped holding its annual meetings. One of its members was supposed to be the representative of the bishopric of Magdeburg, but this bishopric was ruled at the time by a Protestant administrator who had not been enfeoffed by the emperor with the diocese and consequently did not have a seat and a vote in the Imperial diet. As such, it was questionable whether he could be a member of the visitation committee. To prevent the situation from spiraling out of control, the emperor suspended the work of the entire committee and postponed the auditing and reviewing of the Imperial chamber court indefinitely. Because every decision of the court could be reviewed by this same committee, however, the work of the entire court ground to a halt when the committee was suspended. A majority decision by the Imperial diet to make an exception and entrust the visitation of the Imperial chamber court to an ad-hoc committee of Imperial deputies failed. The Protestants found themselves in the minority in this committee as well and therefore disputed its authority immediately. The Imperial Aulic council was now the sole functioning supreme Imperial court, but in the eyes of many Protestants in the 1580s and 1590s, its verdicts, too, were tainted by anti-Protestant prejudices. They consequently argued that only the biconfessional Imperial chamber court had jurisdiction over religious questions, and even this only in those cases where the Peace of Augsburg laid down firm and unambiguous rules. In all scenarios not covered explicitly by the peace of 1555, only amicable agreements between the two sides could form the basis for a solution.

In 1603, and for the last time, the Imperial diet approved a special tax for the war against the Ottomans. Five years later, the diet chose to reconvene in Regensburg, hoping that this city's tradition of amicable coexistence between Protestants and Catholics would influence its own proceedings as well. The optimism proved baseless, and the diet quickly reached an impasse because of a series of fundamental procedural disputes. After an extremely disadvantageous peace agreement with the Ottomans in 1606, the emperor laid before the diet yet another request for special taxes, hoping that another campaign in the southeast would turn things in his favor. In return for their approval of the new taxes, the Protestant estates demanded that the emperor reconfirm the Peace of Augsburg. Archduke Ferdinand, who represented the emperor in the diet, was willing to do so, but only if all previous breaches of the peace were rescinded. Had they accepted Ferdinand's offer, the Protestants would have had to agree to return all church property they secularized after 1552. This, of course, they refused to do. Once again, the conflict escalated around the question of the constitutionality of decision by majority. The Protestants left the city, and the diet disassembled without a formal recess.

The longer the confessional conflicts lasted the more intent the two sides became on forging their own military alliances. Immediately after the failure of the Imperial diet of 1608, a group of mostly Calvinist estates formed the Protestant Union. Led by the Palatine elector, the Union was a ten-year defensive alliance with the common purpose of defending its members' rights. The Union had its own treasury and army, and it formed further alliances with foreign Protestant powers. The Catholics did not remain idle either. In June 1609, Duke Maximilian of Bavaria formed the Catholic League, an alliance between Bavaria, the three ecclesiastical electors, and a host of other ecclesiastical principalities, although not with the Habsburgs. Just like the Protestant Union, the Catholic League was defensive in nature, had its own treasury and troops, and aimed to guarantee "the keeping of peace and rights." But unlike the Union, the League also added to its aims the execution of the Imperial diet's decisions, and it was subsidized by the papal curia. In reaction to the formation of the Catholic League, more Protestant estates joined the Protestant Union. The confessional battle lines were forming quickly. When the two sides came again to an Imperial diet in 1613, each presented a long list of demands, and all efforts at reconciliation proved futile. The Catholic majority formulated an Imperial recess without the support of the Protestants, who, on their part, responded by challenging the constitutionality of the whole procedure. Thus disappeared the last remaining platform for reconciliation. An Imperial diet would not reconvene until 1640.

It was exactly at this time that two major European alliances were forming in response to the succession dispute in the duchy of Jülich-Cleves—a large territorial complex on the Lower Rhine. Only a couple of fortunate coincidences prevented this conflict (1609–1614) from escalating into a major war between the different confessional camps in Europe, as would happen only a few years later.

All these confessional conflicts contributed to a growing sense of a looming storm in the Empire. The situation was compounded by the economic consequences of a deteriorating climate (the "Little Ice Age" of the seventeenth century), growing populations, depleted resources, and the consolidation of territorial princes' power in their particular domains. The sense of crisis expressed itself in different ways. Between 1590 and 1620, a series of urban revolts shook the Empire. Just as in the early years of the Reformation, Jews were now also more likely to fall victim to local riots and even pogroms in those few Imperial cities that still hosted them (Speyer in 1603, Worms in 1615, Wetzlar in 1609, and Frankfurt am Main in 1614). It was also at this time that the "witch craze" of the early modern period reached its peak. All these developments were both indications for and factors in creating a combustible political atmosphere. Soon enough, the glowing embers of confessional animosity burst into a horrendously destructive conflagration.

6

THE THIRTY YEARS' WAR AND
THE PEACE OF WESTPHALIA

The name "Thirty Years' War" suggests a homogeneous military conflict over a period of three decades. This is misleading: the war was a cluster of military conflicts that often had little in common with one another. Some of these conflicts had begun well before 1618, while others would continue even after the Peace of Westphalia in 1648. The Dutch-Spanish war, for instance, had started already in 1568, while the Spanish-French conflict would end only in 1659. Nevertheless, already contemporaries viewed this complex set of conflicts as part of the same event, which they termed "the German War." This was an appropriate name, because the war's main theater of operations was indeed the Holy Roman Empire. It was in the Empire that the major European powers chose to pursue their interests by means of military force, and it was in the Empire that the war's atrocities and devastation affected the local population the most—in some regions, two-thirds of the population was wiped out by 1648. Politically, too, the name "German War" is quite appropriate: during the war, it was the very constitution of the Holy Roman Empire that was at stake. At which level would the process of state-building continue in the German lands—that of the Empire as a whole or that of its constituent parts? To what extent was the emperor allowed to use violence against the Imperial estates, and to what extent were such estates allowed to use force against their own estates and subjects? Should the Empire be allowed to evolve into a centralized monarchy with the emperor at its head, or should it be turned into a federative association of largely independent members? The emperor's enemies raised such questions polemically as a supposedly stark choice between "Spanish servitude" and "German liberty." Indeed, the escalating contestation over such constitutional questions was inseparable from the confessional context in which they were posed. The Empire's Protestant members fought for territorial rule over religious questions in their lands (*landesherrliches Kirchenregiment*) and at the same time for their participatory rights on the level of the Empire. The Protestant nobles in the Catholic Habsburg territories fought for their religious autonomy and at the same time for their participatory rights on the level of the territories. The emperor, after all, sought to expand his central monarchical role in the Empire at the expense of the liberties of the Imperial estates. Above all, however, the war lasted so long and had such disastrous consequences because the constitutional conflicts in the Empire intertwined with the larger conflict between the Habsburgs and the French Bourbons over the balance of power in Europe. Other disputes attached themselves to it as well. The Empire's territories lay in the middle of several regional conflicts in which it was either implicated from the start or into which it was slowly drawn because of Habsburg involvement. That was the situation in the northwest through the Dutch revolt against the Spanish Habsburgs; in the Baltic Sea through the conflicting political interests of the kings of Denmark, Sweden, and Poland-Lithuania; in the southeast through the war against the Ottomans and their allies in Hungary as well as through the revolt in Bohemia; and in the south through the centuries-old French-Habsburg conflict over Italy. The last conflict flared up again because of the succession question in Mantua and the dispute over the strategic Lombard region of Valtelinna.

The German War began as a limited, regional rebellion of Protestant estates against their Habsburg lords. In the century before 1618, the Protestant estates in the kingdom of Bohemia had managed to assert their autonomy vis-à-vis their Habsburg kings, and they had even begun a series of independent confessionalization and state-building policies in their individual territories. They used the inner-dynastic rivalry between the Habsburg brothers Rudolf II and Matthias to wrest from Rudolf a formal, written guarantee of their political and religious rights ("Letter of Majesty," 1609). It was on the basis of these rights that the estates later opposed the re-Catholicization attempt of their new king, Ferdinand (who in 1619 would also be elected emperor). In the wake of the defenestration of Prague in 1618—a symbolic act of resistance against the Habsburg stadtholder—the estates of Bohemia, Silesia, Moravia, and Lusatia formed a confederation (*confoederatio bohemica*), which the estates of Lower and Upper Austria soon also joined. Evoking the fact that Bohemia, just like the Holy Roman Empire as a whole, was an elective monarchy, the estates deposed Ferdinand and placed the elector Palatine, Frederick V, on the Bohemian throne—the same Frederick who led the Protestant Union. Ferdinand, the deposed king of Bohemia but soon Holy Roman Emperor (1619–1637), found support with Duke Maximilian of Bavaria, the head of the Catholic League, despite the long-standing rivalry between their respective Catholic dynasties. Also supporting the emperor was the elector of Saxony, a traditional Habsburg ally. In exchange for using the League's forces against the Bohemian rebels, the duke of Bavaria received the emperor's promise not only to keep any lands he might conquer as securities for his military expenditures, but also to receive the electoral vote of the count Palatine (who was also a member of the Wittelsbach dynasty). The Protestant rebellion in Bohemia ultimately failed, partly because other Protestant forces did not support it effectively. Once he subdued the rebellion, Emperor Ferdinand II ordered the spectacular execution of its leaders, dispossessed the entire Protestant elite in Bohemia and deprived it of its political power, re-Catholicized the land's subjects, and abolished in 1627, through the so-called renewed land ordinance (*Verneuerte Landesordnung*), all the special privileges of his Bohemian estates.

For the constitution of the Empire, the outcome of the Bohemian revolt produced momentous consequences. Frederick, the Palatine "Winter King" (so-called because of his short reign as king of Bohemia), became an Imperial outlaw, lost his electorate, and fled to the Netherlands while his allies carried the war to northwestern Germany. Without the consent of the Protestant electors, the duke of Bavaria received the Upper Palatinate, parts of the Lower (electoral) Palatinate, and a hereditary electorate. The Catholics now formed a clear majority in the chamber of electors. This development contributed to the transformation of the conflict from a regional into an Imperial one. The initially secret agreement between the emperor and the duke of Bavaria was constitutionally egregious, because it infringed on one of the oldest constitutional documents in the Empire—the Golden Bull of 1356, which set clear rules for the number and identity of the seven electors. The only precedent for Ferdinand's actions was Charles V's decision in 1548 to transfer the electorate of Saxony from the Ernestine to the Albertine branches of the Wettin dynasty. Already in the emperor's response to the Bohemian revolt one can detect a structural phenomenon that would characterize the remainder of the war. The emperor did not stand at the head of an Imperial army but had to rely on powerful warlords such as the dukes (and then electors) of Bavaria. The latter pursued their own dynastic and personal interests and therefore demanded—and often received—lands, sovereign rights, and an elevated constitutional-political status.

The conflict escalated further in July 1625, when King Christian IV of Denmark intervened in the war on behalf of the Winter King.

As duke of Holstein, Christian was an Imperial member and moreover the strongest prince in the Lower Saxon circle, which the Catholic League's army now threatened to invade. Having been elected by the other estates to head the circle earlier in 1625, Christian justified his conduct by invoking his responsibilities to it. In reality, he simply sought to expand his power along the shores of the Baltic Sea at the expense of his Swedish rivals. This, too, was a structural weakness of the Imperial constitution: the ruler of a neighboring monarchy could simultaneously be an Imperial member. As such, he could use his influence in Imperial institutions in the service of a foreign country.

In 1625, the Winter King finally managed to gain support from other European powers: the Netherlands, England, and Denmark joined forces with him in the Treaty of The Hague. Together with the military commander Count Ernst von Mansfeld, and backed by Prince Gabriel Bethlen of Siebenbürgen, Christian IV then tried to turn the situation in Bohemia back in Frederick's favor. The Catholic League quickly defeated Christian, and he had to conclude the Peace of Lübeck with the emperor in 1629 and leave the war in Germany for good. For the first time, the emperor was able to extend his power all the way up to the Baltic Sea. The northern territories he now controlled had been part of the Empire in the past but, until then, very far, geographically and politically, from the emperor's actual sphere of influence. This changed now: for a brief moment, the emperor seemed the sole master of the situation.

For his unprecedented success, the emperor had to thank both the Catholic League and the general and military entrepreneur Albrecht von Wallenstein. Wallenstein was a lower Bohemian noble who assembled, financed, and led a strong, efficient army by himself. In exchange for his services, the emperor endowed Wallenstein with the duchy of Mecklenburg, an important Imperial territory with a seat and a vote in the Imperial diet. (The emperor had deposed the previous rulers of the duchy owing to their alliance with the Danes.)

Deposing a prince was undoubtedly within the emperor's traditional legal authority, but only as long as the new ruler was a member of the same family. The transfer of Mecklenburg from its former duke to a Catholic and foreign parvenu was consequently seen as egregious. Just like the transfer of the Palatine electorate to Maximilian of Bavaria, Wallenstein's new title was a breach of the Imperial constitution. The emperor simply did not have the authority to make such a transfer unilaterally; the legal and political conventions of the Empire demanded that such a fundamental change to its political and social order be made only with the explicit consent of the Imperial estates. The entire situation represented a political and constitutional paradox: since the estates refused to support the idea of an Imperial army independent of their control, the emperor had no choice but to rely on military entrepreneurs like Wallenstein. The latter, however, demanded to be raised to the rank of Imperial princes and thus undermined the position of the older Imperial estates.

Wallenstein's success owed much to his willingness to let his soldiers subsist on what they could forage in the lands they occupied (the so-called contribution system). Such a system circumvented the often difficult and time-consuming traditional process of persuading the Imperial estates to vote for taxes to fund an Imperial army. Making Wallenstein's system even more effective was the fact that the Imperial estates themselves did not possess standing armies. Their territories were consequently practically defenseless when his troops marched across their borders. This is the reason why, in 1627, even the electors in the emperor's camp began criticizing Wallenstein's methods and tactics and urged the emperor to reduce the number of his general's troops.

Following his many military successes, Emperor Ferdinand II was now at the zenith of his power, which he tried to leverage in revising the confessional and political-constitutional order in the Empire. His idea was similar to Charles V's in the wake of the latter's victory against the Smalkaldic League in 1548: to recalibrate the balance of power in the Empire by endowing the emperor with much more constitutional weight than before. After the conclusion of the Peace of Lübeck in March 1629, Ferdinand consequently released—once again without the consent of the Imperial estates—the Edict of Restitution. The edict interpreted the confessionally contested clauses in the Religious Peace of Augsburg in favor of the Catholic side and declared the *Declaratio Ferdinandea* null and void. In a step that would have meant the restitution of countless abbeys in Protestant territories to their original Catholic rulers, all non-immediate church property in the Empire was to revert to its pre-1552 legal status. The edict further ordered that the Reformed (Calvinist) Imperial estates, which up until then had been tolerated by Lutherans as coreligionists according to the Augsburg Confession, were to be excluded from the protection of the religious peace of 1555. In several principalities, the following years witnessed a rapid succession of restitution measures in the edict's spirit, although these often led to conflicts among the Catholics themselves, because the new religious orders competed with older ones over the restored properties.

The emperor's assault on the religious rights of the Imperial estates faced strong opposition. Even former allies of the emperor like the electors of Saxony and Brandenburg perceived his actions as infringements on their constitutional liberties. They feared that the emperor planned to do in the Empire as a whole what he had already accomplished in Bohemia. Even the Catholic electors—especially Bavaria—were willing to risk a direct confrontation with the emperor over this matter. They used the electors' diet in Regensburg in 1630 to pressure the emperor and to demand that he fire Wallenstein. Ferdinand had to concede on this point, because he needed the electors' support for the election of his son as Roman king. Wallenstein withdrew to his estate in Bohemia, and the emperor's army was reduced by two-thirds and united with the Catholic League's troops. At the same time, the emperor kept insisting on the Edict of Restitution, even though, without Wallenstein's army, he no longer had the means to enforce it. His intransigence eventually cost the emperor the support of the electors of Saxony, Brandenburg, and Bavaria. The first two, despite their different confessions (the elector of Saxony was Lutheran and Brandenburg's was Calvinist), began to pursue common policies (the Leipzig Alliance of 1631), while the third formed a separate alliance with France. From the emperor's perspective at least, the Edict of Restitution proved a complete failure.

In the early 1630s, the ongoing constitutional conflict in the Empire offered an excuse for yet another alien power to intervene in its affairs. King Gustavus Adolphus of Sweden, who had already hatched plans in this direction before the Edict of Restitution, used the publication of the edict as pretext to land in northern Germany in 1630, portraying himself as the defender of German liberties and protector of the Protestants. (The latter, at least at first, did not really appreciate the gesture.) Taking all contemporaries by surprise with his immense successes on the battlefield, and backed by French support (Treaty of Bärwalde, 1631), Gustavus's troops marched rapidly from north to south. Successfully employing new military tactics, the Swedish army invaded one German territory after another: from Pomerania in the north through Electoral Mainz in central Germany, all the way to Bavaria in the south. After an initial hesitation, the Protestant estates joined forces with the Swedish king. Playing an important role in their decision was the brutal siege and burning of the city of Magdeburg by the Catholic League's troops under Count Tilly. When the emperor decided to attack the lands of his former close ally, the elector of Saxony, the latter decided to join the Swedish camp as well. The emperor responded by calling Wallenstein back from retirement and raising a new army, and after Gustavus Adolphus fell in the Battle of Lützen (1632), the tide of war turned once again and the Swedish forces began to withdraw. A year later, in 1633, the Protestant estates of the four southern German Imperial circles formed a major alliance with Sweden, the Heilbronn League, which jeopardized Electoral Saxony's position as the head of the Protestant camp. After the emperor became suspicious of Wallenstein's loyalty, he had him assassinated. Then, supported by Bavarian and Spanish troops, he engaged the Heilbronn League in a pitched battle outside the city of Nördlingen (Swabia). His victory in the battle was decisive.

This time the emperor avoided the mistake he had committed in 1629 with the Edict of Restitution. His aim, above all, was to bring peace and unity to the battered Empire. Unlike in the past, he now understood that he could assert his power and prevent the Empire from falling victim to the schemes of foreign powers only by collaborating with, and protecting the rights of, its powerful princes. That was the reason the emperor concluded the Peace of Prague with the elector of Saxony (1635), to which in the following years almost all other Imperial estates added their signatures. The Peace of Prague called for the dissolution of all existing military alliances in the Empire—especially the Catholic League—and the transfer of their troops into a single army under the overall command of the emperor. Within that army, however, each Imperial estate would continue to maintain and command its own contingent. The signatories further agreed to expel all foreign forces from the Empire. In terms of the Empire's confessional-legal arrangements, the Peace of Prague suspended the implementation of the Edict of Restitution by forty years and established the "normal day" (Normaltag) of November 12, 1627 (or November 2, according to the old Julian calendar used by most Protestants). All confessional changes that had taken place after that day were to be null and void. The date agreed to as the Normaltag was a convenient one for the Catholic side because it preceded Gustavus Adolphus's invasion of the Empire, but it was also advantageous for the Protestants because it nullified the emperor's restitution policies after 1629. The Counter-Reformation measures taken by the Habsburgs in their own territories remained unaffected.

The Peace of Prague would have ended the war in Germany had the conflict been only a constitutional and confessional clash between the emperor and the Imperial estates. But by 1635, nothing could prevent foreign powers from continuing to fight each other on German soil. Thus began the final but also the longest and most destructive phase of the war, which turned the German War into a "European War in Germany" (K. Repgen). After 1635, France, led by Louis XIII's chief minister Cardinal Richelieu and allied with the Netherlands and several northern Italian principalities, waged war against Spain. In March 1636, it also declared war against the Holy Roman Emperor, thus drawing the German states into the conflict. For the next twelve years, France was also allied with its confessional rival Sweden against Spain, the emperor, and the Empire as a whole. Military gains by both sides always proved temporary, and the entire strategic situation resulted in a stalemate. Sweden's position in the Empire reached a nadir in 1640, but its chancellor, Axel Oxenstierna, was unwilling to withdraw completely from Germany without territorial and monetary compensation for its sacrifices. Indeed, in 1641 Sweden and France renewed their alliance, agreeing that neither side would conclude a separate peace treaty without the other's consent.

In 1636, Ferdinand II managed to guarantee the election of his son as Roman king and successor. One year later, the old emperor was dead. During the rule of Emperor Ferdinand III (1637–1657), the strategic situation of the Spanish Habsburgs in Europe deteriorated considerably, thus releasing France's military leaders from some of their most pressing engagements and allowing them to concentrate on the events in the Empire. The emperor, pressed militarily by the French and urged on by the Imperial estates, was ready for serious peace negotiations. In 1640, after a hiatus of twenty-six years, he convened an Imperial diet to discuss possible solutions to the confessional and constitutional questions in the Empire. The foreign powers attempted, but ultimately failed, to prevent this diet from taking place.

In the following eight years, the war in Germany continued unabated. Sweden renewed its offensive in Germany; Denmark and Siebenbürgen were drawn into the conflict once again; large armies continued to sow destruction in cities, towns, villages, and the countryside; and the emperor's armies suffered several painful defeats. Hunger, plague, and violence decimated the German population. At the same time, the sides continued to look for a final peace deal. After so many years of military conflict, it was now common knowledge that no side could impose a final settlement unilaterally on all the others: a general peace depended on the involvement of all interested parties. In 1641, representatives of the emperor, France, and Sweden met in Hamburg and reached an agreement about the procedural rules of the peace conference. They chose the cities of Münster and Osnabrück in Westphalia as the two locations for the negotiations. These two wealthy cities were close to each other, had escaped the war's devastation largely unscathed, and belonged to two different confessions—Münster being Catholic while Osnabrück was Lutheran. The need to choose two separate locations for the negotiations was the result of the papal nuncio's refusal to meet in person with Protestants. The peace conference was scheduled originally for March 1642, but France and Sweden postponed its opening because they still hoped to strengthen their respective negotiating positions through successful military campaigns. Gradually, several Imperial estates withdrew from the war by concluding separate peace treaties: Brandenburg in 1641, Braunschweig in 1642, Electoral Saxony in 1643, and Bavaria in 1647. After the emperor's plenipotentiaries had assembled in Westphalia in 1643, other parties began sending their representatives to Münster and Osnabrück as well. They included not only envoys of the warring parties but also the representatives of Venice and the pope, who were to serve as brokers in the negotiations. Simultaneously, the Netherlands and Spain also met in Westphalia. They sought a solution to their eighty-year war and eventually reached a formal agreement that recognized the independence of the United Provinces (the Dutch Republic) from Spain.

Before the peace negotiations could begin in earnest—indeed, before the sides could even meet each other at all—certain procedural issues had to be settled. This was the result, among other things, of the fact that it was in Westphalia that representatives of almost all the European powers assembled together for the first time in a general peace congress. They consequently needed to agree on a ceremonial configuration that would express adequately not only the rank and dignity of the individual participants but also their power relations within the European state system. Such considerations were by no means superfluous, because the ceremonial configurations of the negotiations were themselves an early expression of what the negotiations had to solve—the future political-legal constellation in Europe and the place of the congress's participants in it. It was exactly this issue that made it difficult to figure out how the Empire and its individual members were to participate in the negotiations. Should the emperor alone represent the Empire, either in person or through plenipotentiaries? Should he do so together with the electors, or perhaps with the other Imperial estates as well, and if so, how? Since 1643, the Reichsdeputationstag, the Imperial representative assembly, had been meeting regularly in Frankfurt am Main. Composed of representatives of all the Imperial circles, the assembly aimed to formulate a common Imperial position before the opening of the peace negotiations in Westphalia. The assembled estates demanded independent votes in the upcoming negotiations—which would set an important precedent for how the Empire and its constituent members were represented in peace negotiations and therefore would also be an important political statement about the international-legal status of the Imperial estates and indeed about the very constitution of the Empire. This last issue was especially important, because it touched on the fundamental question of whether one should understand the Empire as a loose federative system of independent members or as a unified monarchy, headed by the emperor but limited by the participation rights of the Imperial estates. France and Sweden embraced the federative conception of the Empire and managed, with the support of some Imperial estates, to push this latter conception through—the Imperial estates ended up sending their own individual representatives to Westphalia. For all these reasons, the negotiations in this unprecedented peace congress proceeded in a rather cumbersome manner. There was no general assembly in Westphalia, only visits by the different delegations to the quarters of their respective interlocutors. The negotiations' piecemeal progress had to be reported back and forth between Münster and Osnabrück as well as between Westphalia and the princes, estates, and cities the delegations represented. Despite the communicative obstacles and the elaborate political mechanisms, the different sides ultimately reached two parallel peace treaties, which they signed on October 24, 1648. The first was between the emperor, the Empire, and Sweden (Instrumentum Pacis Osnaburgense), the second between the emperor and France (Instrumentum Pacis Monasteriense). Everywhere in the Empire, the news of the peace caused much jubilation and public celebration.

The Peace of Westphalia had a Janus face: it was both an international peace treaty and a constitutional arrangement in the Empire itself. Based on a general amnesty for all wrongs committed during the war, the peace satisfied the territorial demands of the great powers, reaffirmed confessional coexistence in the Empire, and struck a new balance between the respective weights of the emperor and the estates in the Imperial constitution.

The Peace of Westphalia reaffirmed the basic principles of the Religious Peace of Augsburg but also settled the ongoing disputes about its ambiguous clauses. Crucially, unlike the Peace of Augsburg, it was not limited in time. The peace conferred the exact same legal status on the different confessions in the Empire, including (unlike in the Peace of Prague in 1635) the Reformed one, and it forbade any future use of violence between Imperial members. The peace further regulated the legal status of the three confessions based on the new Normaltag of January 1, 1624—in other words, it practically rolled back the political, legal, and confessional situation in the Empire to before Wallenstein's conquests and the Swedish invasion, while also legalizing the Protestant secularizations after 1552. It became evident very quickly that such an attempt to turn back the clock was extremely difficult: reconstructing the legal situation of January 1, 1624, a quarter of a century later proved all but impossible. The situation in 1624 itself was not always clear, and there had simply been too many changes to it over the following twenty-four years. The Normaltag regulation also contradicted the ius reformandi of the Imperial estates, principles that the Osnabrück peace treaty also reaffirmed. Only in the Habsburg hereditary lands and the territories belonging to Imperial knights did the peace treaty leave the rulers' ius reformandi completely intact, and the Bavarian Upper Palatinate, it stipulated, would remain Catholic. The Peace of Westphalia reinvested the count Palatine with an electoral vote, although it also let the duke of Bavaria keep his. Thus, there were now eight Imperial electors, as opposed to the previous seven. The Imperial estates (including the cities) retained in principle their rights over religious matters, but with a crucial stipulation that prohibited them from discriminating against subjects of a different confession—such subjects were allowed to continue their religious practice in private, if they wished to do so. The confessionalization process in the Empire consequently ground to a halt. If a ruler decided to convert to a different confession—a common practice in the decades after 1648—his subjects were by no means required to follow his example. Furthermore, the peace did not abolish the ecclesiastical privileges—it continued to protect the ecclesiastical principalities from secularization. Above all, the Peace of Westphalia modified the Imperial institutions in such a way that no confession would have the upper hand. It did so through a parity principle between the two main confessional groups in the Empire (Reformed and Lutherans being considered one confession). Of the fifty assessors in the Imperial chamber court, for instance, twenty-four had to be Protestant. Imperial offices in the biconfessional Imperial cities had to have double occupancy, half Catholic, half Protestant. The constitution of the important bishopric of Osnabrück now dictated a complex biconfessional system in which its territorial lordship would alternate between Catholics and Protestants. But above all, the Imperial diet itself could no longer settle religious questions through a majority decision. In the future, the solution to all such questions had to be based on an amicable agreement between the two confessions. If a religious issue came before the diet, the Catholic and Protestant estates were to withdraw and discuss it separately (*itio in partes*), formulate their respective positions on the matter, then negotiate a consensual decision between them. Thus, the Peace of Westphalia did not make the confessional problem in the Empire disappear once and for all. On the contrary, its mechanisms guaranteed that the confessional divide would be a hallmark of the Imperial constitution for the rest of its existence.

By modifying the internal balance of the Imperial constitution, the Peace of Westphalia set the course for future political developments in Germany. State-building processes in this part of Europe could not be led by the emperor or proceed on the level of the Empire as a whole. Rather, they took place only in the Empire's constituent parts, especially the more powerful among them (including the emperor's own hereditary lands). The peace codified all the hereditary rights, liberties, and privileges of the Imperial estates, their territorial estates, and their subjects; it had a clearly conservative tendency regarding such issues. But it did not stop there. It codified the rights of the Imperial princes to freely exercise their territorial supremacy (*Landeshoheit: ius territoriale*), including the right to form alliances with foreign powers as long as those were not directed against the emperor or the Empire in general. (Such a right could be useful only for those estates that commanded their own armies.) This territorial supremacy (*superioritas territorialis*) was not equivalent to a full, internationally recognized sovereignty in the modern sense of the term, because the Imperial estates still had feudal obligations toward the emperor (who continued to be their formal lord) as well as toward the Imperial institutions. The very stipulations in the Peace of Westphalia that limited the estates' ius reformandi (at the estates' own consent!) argue forcefully against applying the term "sovereignty" to the Empire's individual territories. Finally, the peace reaffirmed the Imperial estates' collective rights in the Imperial diet as well as in any other major decision concerning the Empire as a whole. The logic behind all these developments was the same: to guarantee that the emperor would never be able again to tilt the balance of power in the Empire in his favor.

The Peace of Westphalia was by no means only a constitutional document for the Empire (even if the next Imperial diet, meeting in 1654, would recognize it as such). It was also an international peace treaty containing a long list of specific diplomatic settlements. It acknowledged once and for all the sovereign status of the Swiss Confederation. It granted France and Sweden, the great victors in the Thirty Years' War, territorial and financial concessions as "war reparations": Sweden received the province of Western Pomerania in northern Germany, the secularized bishoprics of Bremen and Verden, and the accompanying seats and votes in the Imperial diet, while the French king obtained the bishoprics of Metz, Toul, and Verdun as well as the formerly Habsburg lordship rights in Alsace. Both powers served as guarantors of the peace, a role they would later use to exert influence on the Empire's internal affairs. Finally, the peace set an important precedent by allowing rulers to use church property as compensation for territorial losses, a provision applied with particular zeal in Brandenburg.

Even though the Peace of Westphalia did not bring about a final, definitive peace in Europe, it did become the blueprint for a new international system. The treaties of Münster and Osnabrück laid the legal groundwork for, and the basic diplomatic communication forms of, European politics in the following centuries. What later generations of jurists came to call the "Westphalian system" was based on the principle of international equality among the major political actors in Europe. Instead of the complicated hierarchy of authority and power with the pope and emperor at the top, the peace treaties opened the path toward an international community whose members were independent, sovereign states. These states enjoyed equal rights and were not supposed to intervene in each other's internal affairs, especially regarding religious questions. Only the Holy Roman Empire and its members still eluded this sovereignty principle. As for the pope, he refused to acknowledge the treaty because it codified the equal status of the Protestant "heretics" in terms of both the Imperial constitution and the international system.

The classical German historiography of the nineteenth and early twentieth centuries viewed the Peace of Westphalia as a national catastrophe. It claimed that 1648 turned the Holy Roman Empire into a looting ground for the "Western Powers" by smashing it into a thousand political fragments, thus rendering it incapable of survival in the long run. This interpretation was clearly colored by later events, including the Napoleonic Wars, the Franco-Prussian War of 1870–1871, the founding of the Kaiserreich, and especially the Versailles Treaty of 1919. Such a backward-projection of later concerns contributed decisively to the emergence of a one-dimensional interpretation of the history of the Imperial constitution in the early modern period. It is unquestionably true that the constitutional modifications of 1648 brought about structural changes that would later contribute to political polarization, the paralysis of Imperial institutions, and the complete failure of any attempt to form a common military defense for the Empire. At the same time, such an interpretation not only has long prevented historians from recognizing that the Peace of Westphalia helped the emperor to gradually reestablish his authority in the Empire and thus to defend its weaker members from the more aggressive ones; it also obscures the fact that after 1648 the Imperial institutions managed to recover from the war years, consolidate their power, and work rather effectively for the next century and a half.

7

THE WESTPHALIAN ORDER AND THE
RENEWED RISE OF THE EMPEROR

In the course of the seventeenth century, the constitutional structure of the Holy Roman Empire became a topic of intensive scholarly
debate. In many publications, legal experts discussed the question of
who exactly possessed the highest authority (*maiestas*) in the Empire. It was above all Jean Bodin, the French jurist and historian, who
helped launch this debate through the novel interpretation of the
concept of sovereignty he developed in his *Six livres de la République*
(1586). In the wake of Bodin's work, sovereignty came to mean an
absolute, uniform, indivisible, and supreme authority that character-
izes all political bodies (*res publica*) as such. The answer to the question of who held sovereignty in a particular case characterized the
form of that *res publica*.

Bodin's work started a long debate about the nature of the Imperial constitution. Some jurists claimed that in the Holy Roman Empire sovereignty rested with the emperor alone, while others favored
the idea that it was in the hands of the Imperial estates as a group
(that is, in the Imperial diet), and yet a third group advanced the
position that only individual princes in the Empire could lay claim
to it. Each attempt to define the relationship between sovereignty

and the Imperial constitution rested on a different conception of what the Empire actually was—a monarchy, an aristocracy, or a federation of independent states, respectively—and each was related to the political interests of its proponents. Because all simple answers to the question of Imperial sovereignty proved unconvincing, jurists began to distinguish between two forms of supreme authority in the Empire—*maiestas personalis* and *maiestas realis*. The emperor, jurists now claimed, possessed the highest personal majesty, but the real supreme authority lay with the Imperial diet. This formulation, too, proved unsatisfactory. The debate dragged on well into the eighteenth century and occupied generations of scholars. It also served as a catalyst for the creation of an entire field of jurisprudence known as "public law of the Roman-German Empire" (*ius publicum Imperii Romano-Germanici*).

Ultimately, all attempts to squeeze the Empire into the general categories of early modern political science added little to its proper understanding. Bodin's concept of sovereignty relied on theoretical abstractions that bore little resemblance to the highly complex historical structure of the Holy Roman Empire. After all, throughout its history one of the main characteristics of the Empire was that it lacked a unified, supreme authority. Rather, it was a hierarchical polity made of interwoven legal rights, where multiple persons and corporations exercised various degrees of power. Gauged by the measuring stick of modern sovereignty, the Empire seemed like a monstrosity, as Samuel Pufendorf famously claimed in 1667. Only later, in the course of the eighteenth century, did scholars grow tired of attempts to find an unequivocal answer to the question of Imperial sovereignty. Thus, Johann Jakob Moser, the great eighteenth-century jurist, called for replacing abstract legal definitions with a detailed and exact description of all the Empire's legal norms and rules. Along the way, he coined the Solomonic phrase "Teutschland wird auf Teusch regirt" ("Germany is ruled in German")—that is, the

Empire should be understood on its own terms, not in the abstract. The continuation of the scholarly debate about the constitutional structure of the Holy Roman Empire mirrored the general political conflict in Germany at the time. On one side stood the large Imperial estates, which increasingly resembled modern sovereign states, while on the other was the Empire, which grew slowly over the course of many centuries and still retained many of its medieval characteristics. In the decades after the Peace of Westphalia, the structure of the Imperial constitution was not just the topic of abstract scholarly debates; practically, too, it remained unclear whether the Empire would retain its hierarchical structure, with the emperor and the electors at its head, or evolve into a loose confederation of largely autonomous princely states.

The Peace of Westphalia stabilized the conditions under which state-building processes could proceed in the large Imperial estates. For a long time, historians directed almost all their attention to this process and especially to the rise of Brandenburg-Prussia and the success of its rulers' absolutist policies. It is true that several German princes managed to hollow out the hierarchical, estates-based political system in their territories by raising the tax burden on their subjects, expanding state bureaucracies, and creating strong standing armies. Brandenburg-Prussia—as well as Bavaria, Electoral Saxony, and Braunschweig-Lüneburg (which became Electoral Hanover after 1692)—justified such policies by the need to compete with other European powers that pursued similar policies. The strong political position of these territories' rulers had less and less to do with their status within the Empire. Aside from the notable exception of Bavaria, they all acquired the crowns of foreign countries, then acted as "crowned heads" on the same level as their European peers (p. 33). In the long run, this development contributed to the dissolution of the Empire. At the same time, the political order encoded by the treaties of 1648 also secured the preexisting legal constellation in the Empire and froze it, as it were, for the next century and a half. The

Empire helped maintain its members' legal rights, and it became the guarantor for the continuing existence of its weaker estates: the many Imperial bishoprics and abbeys, the countships, the cantonlike territories of the Imperial knights, and the Imperial cities. The Empire's ability to protect the more vulnerable among its members was related to its delicate political balance after 1648. Two main groups faced each other: the Habsburg emperors with the many small Catholic and ecclesiastical estates, on the one hand, and the strong temporal princes, on the other hand. The enormous dependence of the many small Imperial estates on the protection of the emperor created a large (and, from a Habsburg perspective, highly profitable) clientele base for the emperor. Leopold I (1658–1705) used this situation to strengthen his position in the Empire, while Joseph I (1705–1711) and Charles VI (1711–1740) used it in the service of Austrian (rather than Imperial) foreign policy.

No one could foresee these developments back in 1648. The Peace of Westphalia left a series of constitutional issues unresolved (*negotia remissa*), and an Imperial diet assembled in 1653–1654 to address them. Most important was the attempt by some temporal princes, such as the landgrave of Hesse-Kassel and the duke of Braunschweig-Lüneburg, to abolish the prerogatives of the electors—their *Präeminenz* (preeminence)—and turn the Empire into a more loosely structured political association of members with equal rights. The Imperial princes wanted to have a say in the election of new Roman kings, the formulation of a permanent elective capitulation, decisions about Imperial bans, and so on. Other constitutional debates revolved around the exact implementation of the principle of confessional parity in the Imperial institutions, the long-standing concerns about the efficiency of the Imperial chamber court, taxation reform, and the organization of a general Imperial defense. The diet failed to resolve most of these issues, but it did manage to reach an agreement about two cardinal questions that helped highlight the independence of the Empire's most powerful members from all the rest. First, the diet resolved to reject the majority principle in taxation questions. Because a general tax was crucial for the implementation of any general, Empire-wide defense policy, this resolution prevented the Empire from operating in a unified manner in this respect and allowed single members to opt out from the defense of the Empire as a whole. A second resolution by the diet of 1653–1654 obliged the territorial estates to pay Imperial and circle taxes as well as to provide their rulers with the necessary means for their territories' defense. This resolution dealt a crushing blow to the territorial estates' traditional rights vis-à-vis their respective lords, although a later attempt also to prohibit the territorial estates from appealing to Imperial courts in taxation questions proved unsuccessful. The Imperial recess of 1654, which discussed these questions, would come to be known later as the "last Imperial recess" (Jüngster Reichsabschied), because it was the last time an Imperial diet recessed. As it turned out, the next diet after 1654 would never recess formally. Strictly speaking, it would continue to be in session without interruption until the final dissolution of the Empire in the early nineteenth century (pp. 114–115).

The death of Emperor Ferdinand III in 1657 left the question of the Imperial succession open. The old emperor had crowned his only son, Ferdinand IV, Roman king in 1653, but the latter died shortly thereafter. When it came to the election of Emperor Ferdinand's brother Leopold to the Imperial throne, the Imperial estates were most concerned about securing the Peace of Westphalia. They felt that the peace was on shaky ground because of the Austrian Habsburgs' involvement in the war between the Spanish branch of their dynasty and France. The energetic leader of the Imperial estates at this point in time was the elector of Mainz and Imperial archchancellor John Philip von Schönborn, a scion of a modest family of Imperial knights whose members had managed over time to reach the highest political echelon in the Empire through various positions in the Imperial church. Schönborn helped form an anti-Habsburg, multiconfessional alliance (later known as the First Confederation of the Rhine) between a series of Imperial estates and France. The estates feared infringements on their rights by the Habsburgs, but by putting their confidence in France they were trusting the cat to keep the cream. In his electoral capitulations, Leopold had to promise not to form any alliance against France, especially not with his Spanish relatives.

When Leopold I ascended to the Imperial throne in 1658, it looked as if nothing could rescue him from his weak political position. Almost immediately, however, Leopold began pursuing Imperial policies that, in the long run, proved very effective, while also dexterously using the office of the emperor to advance particular Habsburg interests. Two external threats to the Empire formed the general context for Leopold's successes. The first came from the west in the form of Louis XIV's extreme expansionist policies. After 1667, the "Sun King" engaged in a long series of conflicts along France's eastern and northeastern borders, including the Dutch War of 1672–1678, concluded by the Peace of Nijmegen; the "reunions" of supposedly French provinces after 1679; the War of the League of Augsburg between 1688 and 1697, concluded by the Treaty of Ryswick; and the great War of Spanish Succession between 1701 and 1713–1714, which pitted the French Bourbons, Austrian Habsburgs, and Bavarian Wittelsbachs against each other and was concluded by the peace treaties of Utrecht, Rastatt, and Baden. As in the past, some Imperial estates (for example, Bavaria) actually fought on France's side during this time. The second threat to the Empire came from the opposite direction. After the 1660s, the old conflict with the Ottomans flared up again, culminating in the second siege of Vienna in 1683. Following the failed siege, the "Holy Alliance" between the emperor, Russia, Poland, Venice, and the pope managed to achieve a series of spectacular victories against the Ottomans, who, by 1739, had been pushed back from most of their European possessions and ceased to pose a serious military threat. The Austrian Habsburgs were the big winners in the so-called Turkish Wars, since they brought Hungary and large parts of the Balkans under their control. Even the wars against France, which entailed substantial losses to the Empire, eventually helped strengthen the Habsburgs' position. The Empire had to formally concede Lorraine and the important Imperial city of Strasbourg to France, the Palatinate was devastated, and the Habsburgs lost the Spanish crown to their Bourbon rivals. At the same time, the treaties of Rastatt and Baden transferred to the Habsburgs the Spanish Netherlands (modern-day Belgium) and the Spanish possessions in Italy (Naples, Milan, Mantua, and Sardinia). The two external threats to the post-Westphalian Empire consequently had a Janus face. On the one hand, they strengthened the position of the Austrian Habsburgs within the European state system as well as within the Holy Roman Empire. On the other hand, they also highlighted the tension between the emperor's office and the interests of his dynasty on the international stage. Habsburg interests, now more than ever, lay outside the Empire, in Italy and the Balkans.

The successes of the Habsburg emperors against the Ottomans were not the only reason for their strengthened position after 1648. (As the Turkish Wars unfolded, they became spectacular media events that greatly enhanced the Habsburgs' popularity.) It was also based on Leopold's skilled handling of Imperial politics, through which he aimed, and succeeded, at binding the small Imperial estates to his cause. Even some of the more powerful princes in the Empire were now more loyal to the emperor than before. Leopold used his position as the supreme source of legitimacy and social rank in the Empire to augment his revenues and influence. He did so very effectively by making frequent use of his reservation rights (*Reservatrechte*) to upgrade the social status of individuals. The symbolic capital of social rank, estate, and honor was incredibly important in the premodern world, and it strengthened the position of the emperor considerably that he alone possessed the power to augment it (even if, over time, his power, too, was restricted in this regard). Thus, Leopold bestowed an electorate on Braunschweig-Lüneburg in 1692, recognized the raising of Brandenburg-Prussia to the status of a kingdom in 1701, and supported the acquisition of the Polish crown by the elector of Saxony in 1697. These acts were anything but altruistic—Leopold received substantial sums of money for his consent or support in these and other cases. The emperor also pursued very effectively a system of marriage alliances in order to pledge the important dynasties in the Empire to his cause. And he turned his court in Vienna into a glamorous political and cultural center that made government positions there very attractive to the Imperial nobility—even if such positions did not always carry a salary and were in fact very costly to maintain. Leopold also opened many positions in his army to Imperial nobles, giving them the opportunity to acquire not only fame and honor but also their own (physical) estates. Above all, Leopold used the emperor's revived influence in the Holy Roman Empire to staff the Imperial church with relatives and other loyal men, especially the minor Catholic nobles, such as counts and knights, who formed his major clientele base. The emperor exercised his influence in Imperial affairs in different ways. He sent special commissioners to elections of bishops; kept permanent and at times extremely influential representatives at all the important German courts and in the majority of the Imperial cities; and exercised decisive influence at the Imperial diet through his personal representative, the *Prinzipalkommissar* (principal commissioner), as well as through the votes of his own house in the chamber of princes. In 1708, he even managed to push through a decision that gave him, as king of Bohemia, a seat and a vote in all electoral assemblies. Previously, as mentioned earlier, the king of Bohemia participated only in the election of a new emperor.

The most important instrument that Leopold used in exercising his supreme authority was the Imperial Aulic council. This council served him not only as a feudal court and as an executive body but also, and especially, as a supreme Imperial court. In 1654, Ferdinand III released a new set of regulations for the council without the consent of the Imperial estates. Therein, the emperor asserted his *votum ad Imperatorem*, that is, the emperor's right, in his role as the supreme Imperial judge, always to utter the final word on any legal matter. The *votum ad Imperatorem* made the emperor into a mediator and adjudicator in legal disputes between two or more Imperial estates, between Imperial estates and their territorial estates, and between lords and subjects in general. In many cases, the Imperial Aulic council appointed special commissioners and established temporary administrations in the territories of princes who threatened to bankrupt their lands through mismanagement. Above all, the emperor strove to defend local estates from absolutist encroachments by their lords, as happened, most spectacularly, in Mecklenburg and Württemberg. Eventually, after a long, protracted struggle, the local estates in the two duchies secured their privileges by signing a special agreement with their rulers (in 1755 and 1770, respectively). One should nonetheless not overestimate the importance of the Imperial Aulic council, which could carry out its verdicts only against the weaker Imperial members. No one, after all, could force the council's decisions on such powerful rulers as the duke of Braunschweig-Lüneburg or the elector of Brandenburg-Prussia.

Even the Imperial diet itself slowly became an instrument for the exercise of the emperor's influence. In 1663, as the Ottoman threat became acute once again, Leopold summoned the diet to the city of Regensburg. Apart from the still-unresolved issues in the Peace of Westphalia (the *negotia remissa*; see p. 109), the diet also still had to contend with the larger reform of the Imperial constitution and, especially, the formulation of permanent electoral capitulations. The negotiations dragged on, and consensual agreement seemed as elusive as ever. Despite this failure, the ongoing negotiations in Regensburg demonstrated that the diet could serve other functions than the ones it had been originally called to perform. It could serve as an information center for the Empire as a whole, as a forum for reaching agreement on external affairs, and especially as a vehicle for the exercise of the emperor's influence on the smaller Imperial members. For that reason, the diet's representatives never formally disassembled, repeatedly extending the diet and almost unknowingly turning it into a permanent institution, or "perpetual diet" (*Immerwährender Reichstag*). This development changed the diet's character in a fundamental way: the emperor and the princes stopped attending it in person, sending representatives instead. Because the major Imperial dynasties accumulated more and more territories in the following decades, and because the weaker Imperial members could not afford a permanent representation in the diet, many of the representatives in Regensburg controlled more than one vote at any given time. From an ad-hoc, ceremonial, and courtly assembly, the Imperial diet evolved into a permanent bureaucratic organ; its highly complex procedures turned into an "arcane body of knowledge" (Karl Otmar von Aretin) accessible only to a handful of legal scholars and the representatives themselves. The diet's function as a legislative body continued only in isolated cases, such as economic issues that pertained to all the Imperial estates. Its last major legislative acts were the artisanal regulations of 1731 and 1772 (*Reichshandwerksordnung*). It was primarily the emperor who profited from the existence of the diet, although Regensburg was neither the only nor the most important forum for his politics. The electors, on the other hand, had the most to lose from the new state of affairs. Between past meetings of Imperial diets, only the chamber of electors possessed the right to assemble and therefore to deal with urgent, Empire-wide political issues. Now, with the diet in Regensburg in perpetual session, the chamber of electors lost this monopoly.

The most important reform attempts undertaken by the perpetual diet in the seventeenth century concerned the Empire's means of defending itself militarily, the *materia securitatis publica*. It was once again Elector John Philip von Schönborn—advised by the philosopher Gottfried Wilhelm Leibniz—who was the moving spirit behind these attempts. Leibniz's radical reform plans, based on his astute analysis of the shortcomings of the Imperial constitution, were not practicable. Schönborn had already tried to organize an efficient Imperial defense through an association of neighboring Imperial circles. Only later in the seventeenth century, in the wake of the French aggression against the Empire's western and northwestern members, did an actual reform of the Empire's military affairs come to pass. The matter had always been politically sensitive: the establishment of an Imperial army with the emperor at its head could lead the latter to abuse his powers—as had already been the case with Charles V and Ferdinand III in the sixteenth and seventeenth centuries, respectively. In the face of France's actions in the west, however, the Imperial diet reached a series of decisions—later to rise to the status of fundamental laws of the Empire—that, taken together, amounted to an Imperial military constitution. These decisions set rules for extraordinary cases in which the raising of Imperial armies would be deemed absolutely necessary. Such military formations would not be the same as standing armies: they would conscript troops from the ten circles according to a particular agreement, stand under the command of an Imperial field marshal, and be sixty thousand men strong. The diet left it to the individual circles to decide how each would raise troops and how much money each of the circles' estates would contribute to the troops' maintenance. To facilitate the financing of the entire reform program, the diet established a general military treasury (*General-Reichs-Kriegs-Cassa*) under the direction of a general war commissioner (*Generalkriegs-kommissar*). Individual circles often established similar (local) institutions. One-fifth of the new army was supposed to come from the Austrian circle—that is, from the emperor himself. The latter, however, kept commanding his troops directly—they were consequently part of the Imperial army only theoretically; in practice they continued to be members of the emperor's personal army. Other "armed estates" soon imitated the emperor and claimed the right to have their own generals at the head of their troops. Brandenburg-Prussia, for instance, whose territories in the Holy Roman Empire extended across several circles, kept all of its troops under a joint command. As a consequence, the military reforms left largely unresolved the important issue of the overall, unified command of the Imperial army and its treasury. The emperor continued to be the supreme warlord in the Empire, but his actions were also restricted by the diet in crucial domains, such as declaring war or appointing generals. The ensuing system was consequently cumbersome and impractical. The declaration of an Imperial war—let alone the actual formation of an Imperial army—lagged far behind a given conflict's actual events, which, as before, continued to be shaped by the actions of individual princes and their personal armies rather than by the Empire and the troops directly under its command.

The reform of the Empire's military defense represented a compromise between the emperor and the Imperial estates. The Imperial army it created lacked two important characteristics that distinguish modern military forces from premodern ones: it did not operate under a unified high command, and it was not a standing army. Throughout the rest of its history, the Empire's military capabilities remained extremely limited. The Empire never possessed a monopoly over the use of force, which is a fundamental characteristic of modern sovereign states.

After the Peace of Westphalia, the Empire's institutions continued to face the challenge of its internal confessional divides. Although the parity rule and the Normaltag of January 1, 1624, determined the confessional map of the Empire down to its minutest details, they could not always address the ever-changing situation on the ground. Some princes ruled over confessionally homogeneous populations, but in other cases a principality contained mixed—and at times outright bizarre—confessional constellations. The dioceses of Minden and Halberstadt, for example, had partly Catholic cathedral chapters but no Catholic bishops, and the control over Osnabrück alternated between a Catholic bishop and a Protestant prince of the Hanover dynasty. In the "condominiums" (*Kondominaten*), two or more princes of different confessions shared political authority with one another, while in the "simultaneous" territories and cities (*Simultaneen; simultaneum religionis exercitium*), different confessional groups alternately used the very same church buildings. Confessional relations continued to be complicated not only where they had been so in the past but also in new places where territorial lords converted from one confession to another, as they often did. Even though converted princes could no longer force the rest of the population to follow their lead, they could still help their confessional brethren—foreign ones, for instance—to come and settle in their lands. Many Imperial estates converted back to Catholicism in the seventeenth and eighteenth centuries, especially side branches of the major Protestant dynasties that were forced to rely on the resources of the Imperial church or the emperor's court. But conversion was by no means restricted to the lower or marginalized nobility. The elector of Saxony converted to Catholicism in order to be crowned king of Poland, and later both the duke of Württemberg and the landgrave of Hesse-Kassel would become Catholic too. The most conflict-ridden situation was in the Palatinate, where the dynastic branch of Pfalz-Neuburg ascended to the throne in 1685 and began a campaign to re-Catholicize the predominantly Protestant local population. This was a clear breach of the Peace of Westphalia. The same occurred, in reverse, in Brandenburg and Braunschweig, where reprisals by the Protestant ruling dynasties against their Catholic subjects almost led to the outbreak of another general confessional conflict in the Empire.

The Peace of Ryswick, which ended the War of the League of Augsburg in 1697, represented another infringement on the Peace of Westphalia. The peace treaty demanded that France withdraw from some of the territories it occupied on the right bank of the

Rhine, but an important clause in it also guaranteed that the re-Catholicization policies of the previous years would not be rolled back. This clause caused many a heated dispute in the following years; from a Protestant perspective, it represented a constant provocation.

Who had the supreme jurisdiction over religious questions in the Holy Roman Empire became an extremely virulent question from the 1720s onward. In the decades following the Peace of Westphalia, religious conflicts between Imperial estates were addressed by an emperor-appointed group of deputies. But in the 1720s, the Protestant estates began to challenge the emperor's role as the supreme judge over such questions and contested the jurisdiction of deputies and the Imperial courts in such matters in general. Only the Imperial diet, they claimed, could address religious issues. According to the Peace of Westphalia, however, the diet could reach decisions about religious questions only through an amicable agreement between the different confessions. The result was often a stalemate. The insistence of the Protestant estates on having the diet address all issues relating to religion (*recursus ad comitia*)—and which issues, after all, were *not* related to religion?—impeded the smooth functioning of the Imperial constitution. Making matters even worse was the Protestant estates' common handling of political issues as a closed *corpus evangelicorum* (the Protestant members of the Imperial diet). In this way, the confessional schism in the Empire increasingly determined the shape of political discussions and prevented consensual solutions, especially when some of the Protestant estates—such as England-Hanover and Brandenburg-Prussia—used the schism to pursue independent political aims on the Imperial and, especially, the international level.

8

POLITICAL POLARIZATION, 1740–1790

In the eighteenth century, the Empire suffered from rising internal tensions that eventually led to its demise. A fundamental political imbalance was building up within it. The powerful Imperial members considered the Empire to be little more than an obstacle in the pursuit of their individual goals, while its weaker members—now more than ever—viewed it as existentially important for their survival. The Empire's fundamental laws and institutions were the sole protectors of the weaker members' traditional rights, but the powerful Imperial members—including now also the emperor—supported the liberties of the weaker members only insofar as they fit in with their own interests. The more such members were willing to use the Imperial institutions only for their own particular aims, or even to ignore them completely, the less effective was the Imperial constitution. During the eighteenth century, this was the case not only with Brandenburg-Prussia and England-Hanover but also—crucially—with the Habsburgs themselves, because the political center of gravity of all three dynasties now lay outside the Empire. Perhaps the best proof for the declining significance of the Empire in the European state system is the fact that at one point Emperor Francis I (1745–1765) consulted a group of experts about whether the possession of the Imperial crown still brought any advantages at all to the Habsburg dynasty.

Another rising tension in the eighteenth century was between the Empire's overall role as guarantor of peace and justice to all its members and the dynamics of the rapid state-building processes in its large territories. The discrepancy between the "Empire's need and ability to change" (Gabriele Haug-Moritz) became ever more acute. The Peace of Westphalia reaffirmed the rights, liberties, and privileges of the Imperial and territorial estates in all their medieval complexity. At the same time, some of the larger Imperial territories pursued a rapid buildup of quintessentially modern state structures, including the expansion of state jurisdiction into completely new areas. Individual princes often legitimized their actions by invoking the principles of the new rationalistic philosophy characteristic of the seventeenth and eighteenth centuries; they strove to rebuild the state from the ground up according to strictly rational and utilitarian principles. Highlighting the contractual aspect of all political associations, contemporary natural law theory taught that the state's legitimacy rested on its subjects' consent to place themselves under a higher authority in order to better serve the general good. Enlightened philosophers insisted that the state's tasks did not stop at the guaranteeing of peace and law but encompassed also the subjects' "pursuit of happiness." Such a conception was very lucrative to individual princes, because it helped them justify the dissolution of old traditions and privileges that, in their minds, were standing in the way of the rational overhaul of the state. For many enlightened philosophers, the Holy Roman Empire and everything it protected were little more than medieval or "Gothic" structures whose legitimacy was doubtful in the "Age of Reason."

Eighteenth-century critics directed much of their ire against the Empire's ecclesiastical-elective principalities—the Imperial bishoprics and abbeys. They claimed that these principalities lacked governmental continuity and that their elective nature made it easy for neighboring magnates and even the papal curia to intervene in their affairs. Especially problematic in the eyes of Enlightenment-inspired scholars was the fact that the privileged noble canons in the ecclesiastical principalities sometimes used their positions to advance their own selfish interests, receiving various types of "compensations" for their votes and enriching themselves whenever an episcopal see became vacant. More fundamentally, public journals criticized the very connection between ecclesiastical positions and secular possessions, privileges, a courtly lifestyle, and indeed political authority in general. Even Catholic critics now doubted whether ecclesiastical benefices and the salvation of souls were compatible. Enlightened critique did not stop at the ecclesiastical principalities. It encompassed the entire constitutional structure of the Empire, which was, as we saw, most intimately connected with the Church. Even Catholic princes looked on such a critique with a favorable eye. Taking over ecclesiastical properties in their lands could fill their coffers and advance the political unity of their realms. This was the reason why even Catholic princes often threatened to annex and secularize neighboring ecclesiastical territories, abbeys, and collegiate churches.

In the eighteenth century, more and more princes and bureaucrats embraced the new rationalist conceptions of the state. The symbol par excellence of "enlightened rule" for many contemporaries was King Frederick II ("the Great") of Prussia, as well as his Austrian peer, the future emperor Joseph II. Despite the similar policies both men pursued at home, during his long reign Frederick expanded Prussia at Austria's expense, raised it to the status of a great power, and contributed to the polarization of power in the Empire that would eventually bring about its dissolution.

In 1740, Emperor Charles VI died without a male heir. Already in 1713, in a statute known as the Pragmatic Sanction, he had changed the old Habsburg primogeniture succession rules so that his daughter Maria Theresa could inherit his vast lands. The European powers and even the Imperial diet accepted the Pragmatic Sanction in exchange for a series of Habsburg concessions. Nevertheless, when Maria Theresa, who had married Francis Stephan of Lorraine in 1736, ascended to her father's throne as archduchess of Austria and queen of Hungary and Bohemia, her position was immediately challenged. In the early modern period, female regency was always precarious and as such a common cause for contested political claims by side branches of the ruling dynasty, local estates, and neighboring powers. In this case, Frederick II seized the opportunity and, shortly after his own ascension to the throne in 1740, invaded Silesia (just northwest of Bohemia) in a clear breach of Imperial law. Simultaneously, Electoral Saxony and Bavaria claimed parts of the Habsburg lands, which they soon invaded with French support (the War of Austrian Succession, 1740–1748). Several Imperial members were now at war against each other while the Empire as a whole stood on the sidelines.

In 1742, meanwhile, the electors chose a non-Habsburg emperor for the first time in almost three centuries—the Wittelsbach Charles Albert, elector of Bavaria, who would reign as Emperor Charles VII. By 1724, the four Wittelsbach electors of Bavaria, Cologne, Trier, and the Palatinate had formed the Dynastic Union (*Hausunion*), which regulated their mutual relationships as well as their stance vis-à-vis the Holy Roman Empire more generally. Apart from the four Wittelsbach votes in the chamber of electors, Charles Albert's election was also supported by Brandenburg-Prussia and France, two countries that shared a strategic interest in limiting Habsburg influence. Without a strong power base of his own, the new emperor was almost completely dependent on the political and financial support of his more powerful patrons. Despite his majestic coronation in Frankfurt am Main in 1742—staged according to the rules of the old ceremonial protocol—Charles VII lacked the means to execute his office successfully. Because Austrian troops were occupying his capital city of Munich, Charles had no choice but to reign from Frankfurt am Main, a city that now also hosted the Imperial diet. Only when Frederick II reentered the war against Maria Theresa in 1744 did Charles manage to move back to Munich. How damaging it was for the Empire that the emperor lacked a sufficiently independent power base was made clear by some of Charles VII's actions. Supported by Frederick II, Charles planned to secularize the independent ecclesiastical principalities in and around his territories and to annex them to his lands, together with the Imperial cities of Regensburg, Augsburg, and Ulm. The Roman-German emperor planned, in other words, to dissolve some of the Empire's most illustrious members who also formed his very clientele base. Such a plan was tantamount to a betrayal of the emperor's office, whose legitimacy, after all, rested on the emperor's role as guarantor of peace, law, and the hereditary rights and liberties of the less powerful among the Imperial members. All of this led to a massive loss of credibility for Charles in particular and for the emperor's office in general.

After Charles VII's death in January 1745, there was no alternative to the election of Francis Stephen of Lorraine (Maria Theresa's husband) as Roman-German emperor. Only he, it was believed, controlled sufficient dynastic resources to protect the interests of the Empire against powerful neighboring countries such as France. With only Brandenburg and the count Palatine objecting, the electors chose Francis Stephan to be the new Holy Roman Emperor, Francis I, in September 1745. Nevertheless, as the ensuing crisis of Imperial enfeoffment demonstrated soon enough, the emperor's loss of authority in the previous years could not be undone. The renewal of the princes' feudal obligations to the emperor was an old medieval ceremony. It involved genuflection and oaths by the princes (or their envoys) in front of the Imperial throne, a symbolic act of the princes' personal fealty to the emperor intended to affirm that the source of their authority was the Empire itself. Such medieval relations were no longer in line with some of the territorial princes' perception of themselves as independent actors on the European stage. Charles VII had made a secret pact with Frederick II according to which the latter was no longer required to receive Brandenburg as a fief from the emperor. When the pact became public, other electors and princes demanded the same. It was more than a mere symptom of the Empire's decline that from this point on none of the major territorial princes in the Empire renewed their enfeoffment in Vienna, even when they were promised a series of exemptions from other ceremonial practices in return. Indeed, the longer the emperor failed to force the ritual of enfeoffment on the electors and the Imperial princes, the more evident was his political impotence.

The political opposition between Prussia and Austria became increasingly interwoven with the Empire's confessional divide. The Imperial estates in northern Germany were predominantly Protestant, while the majority in the south—especially among the smaller principalities—were Catholic. Prussia used this situation to its advantage by drawing an increasing number of the small Protestant estates into its sphere of influence, even though these estates had previously pursued divergent political goals. In the Protestant north, Prussia had already controlled many of the delegates to the Imperial diet and local assemblies, and it exerted decisive political influence over the rest of the minor principalities. Because decisions in the *corpus evangelicorum* were reached through the majority principle, and because Prussia controlled a majority of the corpus's representatives, it practically controlled the whole body. It was consequently in Prussia's best interest to turn any political issue in the Empire into a religious one and tackle it through the Imperial diet. This instrumentalization of the *itio in partes* (see p.102) quickly paralyzed the diet's proceedings and led to its rapid decline as a forum for the settlement of political disputes.

Frederick II used the Empire's confessional divide to his advantage during the global conflict known in Europe as the Seven Years'

War between 1756 and 1763. (In North America, this conflict is known as the French and Indian War.) The conflict was the consequence of the dramatic collapse of the old alliance system in Europe. To regain Silesia, Austria signed a tripartite agreement with its old rival France and the rising Russian Empire, while Prussia formed an alliance with England-Hanover. In this way, the rivalry between Austria and Prussia fused into the larger conflict between France and England over their respective Atlantic empires. Frederick II began the war by invading Electoral Saxony, whose military and economic resources he hoped to use in his conflict with Austria. The Prussians viewed the war as a conflict between two independent sovereigns— the king of Prussia and the queen of Hungary and Bohemia, respectively—that had nothing to do with the Empire itself. Despite the fact that his first act of war was against a Protestant province (Electoral Saxony), Frederick managed to persuade public opinion that he was waging the war against Austria, France, and Russia in the name of the Protestant cause. Confession was "a vehicle which promised mobilization and unconditional solidarity" (Georg Schmidt) to the other Protestant estates in the Empire. This, together with Maria Theresa's surprising diplomatic coup to form an alliance with France (perceived as the Empire's traditional enemy), explains why it was so difficult for the empress to mobilize the Empire as a whole against Frederick's aggressions. Her first attempt to place Frederick under Imperial ban failed owing to the opposition of the Protestant estates. Only after much effort did the empress finally manage to find a majority in the Imperial diet for raising an Imperial army and launching a military expedition against Prussia's invasion of Saxony. In general, the Seven Years' War highlighted the structural weakness of the Empire as a body capable of effective political and military action. At first, the Imperial estates' interests in the conflict were not aligned with one another's, and even later, when they agreed to enter the conflict, their disagreements prevented a general and efficient military response by the Empire as such. One by one, individual estates concluded separate peace treaties with Prussia and withdrew from the conflict. Finally, just before the end of the war, the Protestant majority in the Imperial diet managed to declare the Empire neutral in the conflict once again. Ultimately, the Empire's confessional divide prevented it from forging a general policy against peace-breaching Prussia, whose control over Silesia was reaffirmed in the Peace of Hubertusburg in February 1763.

Joseph, the son of Francis I and Maria Theresa, had to rule the Habsburg hereditary lands together with his mother from 1765 until her death in 1780. In the Empire, however, the situation was different. A year after the Peace of Hubertusburg, Emperor Francis I had his son crowned Roman king in Frankfurt am Main. When Francis died one year later (1765), Joseph succeeded him to the Imperial throne, while in the Habsburg lands he remained his strict mother's coregent. Joseph II's coronation as king is famous because Johann Wolfgang von Goethe, the celebrated poet, watched its intricate ceremonies as a child and depicted it later in his autobiography. Goethe's description is a highly stylized portrayal of the coronation as a symbol for the declining state of the Empire. Goethe writes in his autobiography that, for a brief moment, the medieval coronation ritual had "revived the German Empire, almost asphyxiated by so many parchments, papers, and books." That Goethe remembered the coronation ritual as anachronistic had to do with the poet's hindsight later in life. Joseph was a political rationalist who based his actions on cold, utilitarian calculations rather than on the Holy Roman Empire's ancient traditions. In his Habsburg hereditary lands, he pursued a radical reform program, dissolving ancient rights and privileges and asserting his superiority over the Imperial church. The Palatine and Bavarian elector (the two electorates were united in the person of Charles Theodore between 1777 and 1799) pursued similar (if not identical) policies by establishing an independent Apostolic nunciature in Munich in 1784. Such a permanent papal representation effectively separated Bavaria from the Imperial church.

These and similar actions by Joseph II and Charles Theodore stood in stark contrast to the program formulated by the suffragan bishop of Trier, Johann Nikolaus von Hontheim (who wrote under the pseudonym Febronius). Febronius's program, which caused a great stir when it was published in 1763, called for the independence of the Imperial church from the papal curia and, should favorable circumstances present themselves, for an ultimate solution to the confessional divide in the Empire. The conflicting interests of the various actors in this drama caused endless disputes between archbishops, bishops, and princes over the structure of the Imperial church and its relationship with the pope. Ultimately, all attempts to reform the Imperial church proved futile because of the tendency of territorial princes to establish their own independent state churches at its expense.

Joseph II started his reign as emperor by pursuing the same enlightened policies he would later try to implement in his hereditary lands. The Holy Roman Empire, however, would simply not yield to his rationalist reforms. This became clear, for instance, in Joseph's failed attempt at a thorough visitation of the Imperial chamber court between 1767 and 1776. The court's problems were many. It was chronically underfunded; the assessors were overburdened by work to such an extent that they allegedly would consider a case only if bribed; the trial procedures were immensely complicated and time-consuming; and the court's verdicts were all but impossible to implement, especially because appealing the court's decision to the Imperial diet became an established practice. The goal of the court's first regular visitation committee in more than 150 years was to control the Imperial chamber court's finances, collect outstanding debts, bring some order into the court's complicated procedures, and cleanse it from abuses and misconduct by the assessors. Although the committee itself was biconfessional, its work was blocked at every turn by confessional divides and by the diverse interests of the different Imperial estates. A clear symptom of the Empire's inability

Figure 4. Audience at the Imperial chamber court in Speyer, 1668. Engraving. *Source*: Pfälzische Landesbibliothek Speyer, Sign. 30 264 Rara.

to undergo reform was the quick escalation of arguments about seemingly trivial details into widespread constitutional conflicts that made any kind of common action all but impossible. In the work of both the Imperial chamber court's visitation committee and other Imperial institutions (including the diet), it was especially conflicts over ceremonial questions, seating arrangements, and titles that stultified important processes, sometimes for many years. For the smaller Imperial members, such questions were nevertheless anything but trivial: legally and politically, they were of the essence, because they touched on the fundamental issues of the minor Imperial estates' independent status and mutual relations.

Faced with the sluggishness of the Imperial institutions, Joseph II turned away from the Empire's politics and concentrated instead on the European interests of the Habsburg dynasty. His lack of concern for the ancient Imperial traditions and laws dealt a fatal blow to the Empire. It was the emperor, after all, who served as the supreme protector of the Imperial members—indeed, the very legitimacy and authority of his office were based on it. By giving up on his responsibilities as emperor, Joseph was hollowing out the office.

All of this was especially evident in the case of the Bavarian succession, which, like so many succession disputes at the time, ended in an armed conflict. In 1777, the last male member of the Bavarian branch of the Wittelsbach dynasty died without an heir. The dynasty's succession rules dictated that the Palatine branch would inherit Bavaria, thus uniting in one person—for the first time in 150 years—the Bavarian and Palatine electorates. Joseph II claimed parts of the Bavarian lands as his own and offered Elector Charles Theodore an exchange of Bavaria for the (Habsburg) Low Countries. Such "land haggling" (as public opinion pilloried the practice at the time) was anything but unusual in eighteenth-century dynastic politics—it had already been exercised in Poland and Lorraine, for instance. Joseph, however, decided to breach Imperial law and invade Bavaria without waiting for the results of the negotiations. The Wittelsbach dynastic branch of Pfalz-Zweibrücken called Frederick II for assistance. The resulting conflict, known as the Bavarian War of Succession (1778–1779), offered Frederick an opportunity to act against the Habsburg emperor in the name of the Imperial constitution. The Treaty of Teschen, brokered by Russia, brought the conflict to an end. As in 1648, a foreign power served as the guarantor of peace.

In 1785, Frederick II had another opportunity to play the role of protector of the Imperial constitution and the Empire's weaker members. With the Bavarian-Habsburg land exchange project still on the table, Frederick formed the League of Princes (*Fürstenbund*), an alliance with a series of small and midsize Imperial estates, including even the Imperial archchancellor, the elector of Mainz. For Frederick II's allies, the issue at hand was the protection of their independence, while for Frederick himself the alliance served primarily as a counterweight to Habsburg power in the Empire. He had no genuine interest in actually reforming the Empire or any of its institutions.

With the deaths of Frederick II in 1786 and Joseph II in 1790, the political situation in the Holy Roman Empire became thoroughly polarized. The Austrian-Prussian dualism affected every aspect of the Imperial constitution, and its opposing gravitational pulls, combined with the cynical confessional politics of both sides, tore apart the Empire's institutional fabric. The weaker Imperial members could not extricate themselves from this polarization and had to choose sides. The powerful Imperial members had long ceased to base their authority and legitimacy on the Empire and consequently had no interests in the Empire as such. Thus, when the continuing existence of the Empire served their particular political goal, they supported it, but when it did not, they showed no qualms in attacking or abusing it. At the end of the eighteenth century, all that was needed for the ultimate collapse of the Empire was one final external push.

9

THE DISSOLUTION OF THE EMPIRE, 1790–1806

On July 14, 1792, the third anniversary of the storming of the Bastille, Emperor Francis II ascended to the Imperial throne. His coronation in Frankfurt am Main followed all the old medieval ceremonial forms, a striking contrast to the events in contemporary France. The reactions in Germany to the French Revolution were nevertheless uneven. Some contemporaries waxed enthusiastic about the French fight for liberty, hoping for similar developments east of the Rhine, including the end of traditional privileges and the old "Gothic" political structures that Imperial law had for so long helped to sustain. On a more theoretical level, the developments in France challenged traditional understandings of what a "constitution" was or should be. There were several regional riots, for example in Lüttich in 1789 and in Electoral Saxony in 1790. Others viewed the situation differently and felt strengthened in their belief in the Imperial constitution: the unfolding fight for liberty in France, they claimed, had been concluded in the Empire and its territories already during the Middle Ages when the Imperial estates guaranteed their independence against monarchical despotism. The Imperial constitution limited the emperor's power over the estates, while the power of the estates was held in check by the emperor and the Imperial courts.

That the traditional liberties of the Imperial and territorial estates had little to do with the general concept of liberty espoused by the French revolutionaries was conveniently ignored. Overly optimistic, perhaps, many felt that public opinion and the sheer force of enlightened discourse would ultimately bring forth a successful reform of the Imperial constitution.

Such hopes had a basis in reality. When Emperor Leopold II was still only the grand duke of Tuscany, he supported a project aimed at creating a modern Tuscan constitution. In stark contrast to his brother Joseph II's often unilateral policies, Leopold strove to implement the new constitution by collaborating with the Tuscan people rather than by thrusting it upon them. Leopold died, however, after only two years as emperor (1790–1792). When Leopold's son, Francis II, ascended to the Imperial throne, the political situation in Europe had deteriorated and the Empire was threatened by war. Prussia and Austria had already concluded a defensive treaty in 1790. When the French National Convention declared war on Austria in April 1792, the two former German rivals thought that they could quickly make political gains while also protecting their aristocratic peers in France (the War of the First Coalition, 1792–1797). After initial successes, the coalition forces suffered a defeat in the Battle of Valmy on September 20, 1792. The emperor urged the Imperial diet to declare a general war against the nascent French Republic, but the diet took almost a year to comply. Decisive for the diet's ultimate decision was Louis XVI's execution in January 1793, which helped turn German public opinion against the French Revolution.

In the meantime, the military situation in Germany's western provinces was deteriorating. After their victory at Valmy, French troops occupied several Imperial territories on the left bank of the Rhine and made preparations to export the revolution to other parts of Europe. The French National Convention agreed on a program to this effect in December 1792. At first, French attempts to export the revolution were limited to the liberation of Germans from the "yoke of feudalism." An important model for this was the founding in mid-1792 of the "Republic of Mainz" on the soil of the eponymous ecclesiastical electorate. This experiment ended a year later with the entrance of the coalition troops into Mainz and the persecution of the local revolutionaries. Soon enough, German supporters of the French Revolution found out to their dismay that the early French promises of liberation and self-determination were little more than propaganda. Instead of liberating the German subjects, the French began to annex occupied territories in Germany to their new republic. War contributions, the quartering of troops, and violent attacks by French soldiers dampened the initial enthusiasm for the revolution in Germany. Nor did spreading news about the Jacobin reign of terror in Paris help the revolutionary cause. The following years witnessed several new plans for a "German constitution," and sometimes local rioters used French revolutionary symbols for their own purposes. Nothing could hide the fact, however, that the Holy Roman Empire lacked any general, coordinated revolutionary movement.

Toward the end of 1794, the Imperial diet urged the emperor to conclude a peace treaty with France because many of the Empire's smaller estates could no longer support the war effort. Brandenburg-Prussia espoused this cause as well and, concluding a separate peace treaty with France (Peace of Basel, 1795), withdrew from the war completely. Doing so was a clear breach of the Imperial constitution. Not only did Prussia now recognize the French occupation of the left bank of the Rhine, but in exchange for its neutrality in the war, it also received some Imperial territories on the river's right bank. Imperial territories north of the Main River were party to the Treaty of Basel as well. The Empire was now split into two camps: a neutral one in the north and an Austria-dominated one in the south. It took Francis II two more years before he was ready to conclude his own peace treaty with France (Campo Formio, 1797). Even then, however, Francis signed the peace treaty not as the Roman-German emperor but as the king of Hungary and Bohemia. Moreover, he now followed the same anti-constitutional principles laid down in the Peace of Basel: the Habsburgs recognized the annexation of formerly Imperial estates to France in exchange for territorial compensation in the Empire itself. The Imperial diet still sent a delegation to the Peace Congress of Rastatt (1797–1799) with the declared goal of keeping the integrity of the Empire. These attempts proved futile, however, because a new war broke out before the congress could conclude its negotiations.

The new war (the War of the Second Coalition, 1799–1801) ended with a clear victory for France, now led by Napoleon Bonaparte. The policies that Napoleon pursued vis-à-vis the Empire aimed at the creation of a "Third Germany" composed of the midsize Imperial estates as a counterweight to both Austria and Prussia. Russia, which had served as guarantor of internal peace in the Empire since the Treaty of Teschen, cooperated with Napoleon on this point. In many respects, the Peace of Lunéville (1801) only confirmed in writing what had already been the situation on the ground. The Imperial territories on the left bank of the Rhine passed into French hands, while the affected princes (especially those allied with Austria) received in exchange territories on the river's right bank. The Imperial diet appointed an extraordinary delegation (Reichsdeputation) to deal with the exact implementation of the Peace of Lunéville. The deputation included representatives from Mainz, Bohemia, Saxony, Brandenburg, Bavaria, Württemberg, Hesse-Kassel, and the Teutonic Order. Paradoxically, the deputation set out to dissolve some of the most fundamental elements of the Imperial constitution by following the Empire's own legal procedures. It wrote into law the constitutional breaches committed by the powerful Imperial members in the previous decade. On February 25, 1803, the Imperial deputation committee published its final recess (Reichsdeputationshauptschluss), in which it accepted the land swaps dictated by France and Russia.

The Imperial recess of 1803 went well beyond compensating some Imperial members for their lost territories on the Rhine's left bank. Rather, it revolutionized the entire legal structure of territorial possessions. With the Rhine serving as the new official boundary between the Holy Roman Empire and France, the Empire's ecclesiastical estates were dissolved and incorporated into the large and midsize Imperial estates in compensation for their losses on the Rhine's left bank. Only the elector of Mainz, the Imperial archchancellor Charles Theodore von Dalberg, retained his position and even enlarged his territories by the formation of the new principality of Regensburg-Aschaffenburg. The Imperial deputation legitimized all these changes without any consideration of traditional territorial boundaries or legal rights. In this manner, it essentially dissolved the constitution of many territorial principalities as well. Some of France's German allies—for example, Bavaria, Baden, and Württemberg—expanded to between six and nine times their former size. The majority of the Imperial cities lost their autonomy and were annexed by their neighboring princes. All in all, about 110 Imperial estates on the right bank of the Rhine ceased to exist next to many more on the river's left bank, which was now part of France. The Imperial deputation still spared the Imperial knights. It was not long, however, before they too lost their Imperial privileges and independent status. In 1803, the neighboring Imperial princes took possession of the knights' territories without relying on any legal justification whatsoever. Territorial looting was the order of the day.

Apart from the secularization of all but one of the Imperial ecclesiastical estates, the Imperial recess of 1803 also dictated a general secularization of church property—that is, the mediatization of all non-immediate (territorial) abbeys and collegiate church properties and their transfer to territorial states. The territorial states were to use these properties for the financing of religious services, poor relief, and education. The large territories created in 1803 were all confessionally mixed. The Imperial recess codified the confessional situation of 1803 and guaranteed freedom of religion to the territorial states' subjects. The structure of the Catholic Church in the Empire underwent a fundamental transformation: holders of ecclesiastical offices lost their rights, benefices, and privileges as political rulers and were limited to caring for their flock's religious needs. Two important consequences of this were, first, that the lower Imperial nobility lost important sources of revenue and career prospects (as church officials), and second, that the sovereign rights of territorial rulers, who had been limited in the past by the Church, expanded substantially.

The emperor and the Imperial diet formally accepted the Imperial recess, adding their names to a document that undermined the old Imperial constitution through and in the name of the traditional Imperial legal procedures. In this respect, the recess anticipated the way the Empire as a whole would be dissolved three years later. Paradoxically, however, the Imperial deputation recess still did not abolish the Holy Roman Empire as such but in fact highlighted some of its fundamental structural elements. For instance, instead of dissolving the elective emperorship, it added new electors—Württemberg, Baden, Hesse-Kassel, and Salzburg. Be that as it may, the recess signified a "territorial revolution" in favor of the large and midsize states by clearing the way of premodern legal structures that prevented the political modernization of individual territorial states. It took no one by surprise that the larger territorial states used the opportunity to annex the smaller ones; this had been in the cards for quite some time. Facing insurmountable difficulties in organizing an Imperial army, Gottfried Wilhelm Leibniz felt this way already in 1670. "Even Imperial members," Leibniz wrote, "could not hide their satisfaction at seeing the impossibility of mending any part of the Imperial constitution. Hoping to save materials from the falling house in order to build something new with them, they await now a favorable opportunity to give the whole building one last good push, although only in such a way that no one could blame them for it."

After 1803, the final dissolution of the Empire was only a matter of time. In 1804, shortly after Napoleon declared himself emperor of France, Francis II established an Austrian hereditary empire. This made it definitively clear that Francis placed his dynastic identity above the traditional dignity associated with the office of Holy Roman Emperor. He probably did so because he already anticipated the dissolution of the Empire and with it the hollowing out of the office of the emperor as well.

By 1805, during the War of the Third Coalition (1803–1806), several Imperial members, including Bavaria, Baden, and Württemberg, had already fought on the French side against Austria. After suffering a crushing defeat near Austerlitz (December 1805), Francis II signed a peace treaty with France in Pressburg that entailed large territorial losses for Austria in Germany and the further shift of the Habsburgs' political center of gravity outside of the Holy Roman Empire. The electors of Bavaria and Württemberg now assumed royal titles. The midsize states continued to rectify their territories through the mediatization of territories previously held by Imperial counts and knights. Prussia clearly dominated all of northern Germany, while southern Germany came under French protection. Thus, the smaller Imperial members lost all vestiges of their independent political existence. Despite the unfavorable circumstances, Imperial Archchancellor von Dalberg kept fighting for the continued existence of a reduced Empire, a "Third Germany" without Prussia and Austria and possibly with Napoleon as emperor. Dalberg's hopes proved illusory: even in the Third Germany, local princes had no interest in the continued existence of an Empire that limited their sovereignty. Instead, they chose to join the Confederation of the Rhine, an alliance forged by Napoleon on July 1, 1806, and headed by Dalberg himself. Shortly thereafter, Napoleon gave Francis II an ultimatum to abdicate from the Imperial throne, and the members of the Confederation of the Rhine declared in the Imperial diet their formal secession from the Holy Roman Empire. On August 6, 1806, Francis laid down the Imperial crown, declared the Empire dissolved, and absolved all Imperial members of their Imperial and feudal obligations. On that day, the Holy Roman Empire ceased to exist.

10

ONCE AGAIN: WHAT WAS THE HOLY ROMAN EMPIRE?

The Holy Roman Empire was not a state in the modern sense of the term. What was it then? In concluding this brief history of the Empire, let us try to give a positive answer to the question of this political body's unique characteristics. It will be divided into eleven points.

1. The Empire was a political association based on tradition and consensus. Its structure relied partly on old customary rules and procedures and partly on mutual agreements between its members. Top-down statutes had little or no place in such an association, because the Empire lacked a supreme legal authority that could enforce its decisions on all the other members. Legal and political rights in the Empire were either practices surrounded by an aura of antiquity and espoused, uncontested, for a long time on the ground, or consensual agreements between the Imperial members. It was especially the written fundamental laws of the Empire that possessed such a consensual character, although even they were only islands in the midst of the

vast ocean of customary law. The Imperial legal order did not have the character of a systematic and well-organized written constitution. Rather, it was an aggregation of often conflicting laws, rights, privileges, and legal procedures that grew slowly over many centuries.

2. The Holy Roman Empire was a complex set of personal relationships that even as late as the early nineteenth century was still based on mutual, personal bonds of fealty. Throughout the Imperial hierarchy, a network of personal oaths tied members to one another: Imperial vassals to the emperor, territorial estates to their princes, city councils to their communities, peasant subjects to their manorial lords, and so on. Public rituals such as coronations, enfeoffments, homages, inaugurations, oath-swearing ceremonies, and installations of new officers created these mutual bonds and endowed them with legitimacy. Exactly because the Empire was a premodern polity that lacked a systematically codified written constitution, it constantly needed to breathe new life into its body politic by way of symbolic rituals and ceremonies.

3. The Empire was a hierarchically structured polity. Its members were extremely diverse in size and social rank, and they were related to the Empire as a whole in myriad ways. At the top of the hierarchy stood the emperor and the electors, further down were the ecclesiastical and temporal princes, and the cities and knights stood at the bottom. Individual Imperial members ruled over their own subjects, who consequently had only an indirect, mediated relationship with the Empire. The emperor had no direct access to them. The Empire consequently did not impart any form of universal Imperial citizenship on its residents.

4. The Holy Roman Empire was a political association that strove to maintain peace and justice. It had a quintessentially defensive structure. Any entity belonging to the Empire, whether as a recognized Imperial member or just as a mediated estate, stood under the protection of the public peace. As such, one could seek legal assistance from the Imperial courts but also had to contribute—directly or indirectly—to the Empire's finances. Nevertheless, the rights the Empire protected were not uniform or equal. The Imperial legal order was extremely convoluted and encompassed an almost endless catalog of "well-acquired" rights, liberties, and privileges (*wohlerworbene Rechte; iura quaesita*). Legal security—the ability to rely on the stable operation of a legal system—did not function in the Empire in the same way as it does in a modern state. In the latter, it takes shape through the universal enforcement of general legal norms, while in the Holy Roman Empire it relied on the historical difference between various legal entities. Throughout the early modern period, the Empire was characterized by increased juridification: parties to political conflicts reverted increasingly to courts of law to settle their differences. At the same time, juridification made it extremely difficult to change the Imperial legal traditions—whether these were based on customary law or on written documents. This situation made it all but impossible to reform the Imperial institutions, especially in the eighteenth century.

5. The Empire was an association of estates and corporations. Already in the late Middle Ages, because large groups could often protect their common rights much better than individuals, all those who enjoyed the same privileges and liberties often formed corporations or estates for the pro-

tection of their common interests vis-à-vis their ruler. "Estates" in the political sense were groups of persons who enjoyed the same rights, shared the same political obligations, and pursued their common interests in an organized manner, for example, through membership in the chambers of the Imperial diet, the territorial assemblies, and urban or knightly diets.

6. The political and social aspects of the Imperial constitution were closely intertwined. The relationships between the different Imperial members were not abstract or anonymous, as they are in modern organizations. To a large extent, they still relied on physical proximity, face-to-face interaction, familial relationships, and patronage networks. Personal, dynastic, and corporative honor were essential motives in political action.

7. The religious and political aspects of the Imperial constitution were also not independent from one another. True, in two crucial moments in the early modern period—1555 and 1648—the Imperial diet codified confessional coexistence in the Empire. But these codifications did not diminish the political significance of the confessions by turning religion into each individual's private business. On the contrary, through the parity principle, the confessional schism saturated Imperial politics through and through.

8. The Holy Roman Empire was a body politic composed of heterogeneous members under the supreme authority of a "head"—the emperor. It was structurally crucial in this respect that the political balance of power between the emperor and the members leaned only slightly in favor of the former. The emperor possessed only authoritative power: he was the head that imparted legitimacy on the

entire Imperial body politic, but he did not have the means to impose his will unilaterally on other Imperial members without relying on his own dynastic power base. All attempts by early modern emperors to form a centralized political power over and against the Imperial estates ended in failure. The coherence of the Empire as a whole was possible only when (and as long as) the powerful Imperial members had an interest in keeping it that way. The diversity among the Imperial members in power, size, rank, and legal status led to different members having very different interests regarding the Empire's political unity. Solidarity among the different Imperial members was an existential matter for the smaller and midsize among them, while the larger members viewed it as useful in some situations and as bothersome in others. Such conflicting attitudes toward the Empire as a whole multiplied rapidly in the course of the early modern period. The more the larger territorial states shifted their political center of gravity outside the Empire, the more the Empire lost on political unity.

9. The Empire's limited political unity, its members' often conflicting interests, and even its sheer size all led to the creation of short-term federative associations that often crossed estate lines. Such regionally or confessionally oriented alliances—from the Swabian League through the Protestant Union and Catholic League, to the League of Princes—decisively shaped the history of the early modern Holy Roman Empire. Individual Imperial circles, as well as regional associations among several of them, had the same character. Such associations helped overcome the weakness of the Empire's central institutions as well as those of specific Imperial members. At the same time, they often undermined general Imperial policies (especially when

foreign powers were also involved) and contributed to the creation of opposing camps within the Empire.

10. The Empire's difficulties in enforcing its authority were the direct result of the general balance of power between its most powerful members. The Empire possessed no executive organs independent from the Imperial estates. Many procedures for settling disputes among Imperial members and between such members and their vassals and subjects—through special commissions appointed by the emperor, for instance, or through the circles' executive organs—functioned well only as long as they did not affect the interests of the powerful Imperial members. When such members opposed central decisions by the Imperial diet or any other Imperial institution, it was all but impossible to force them to change their minds. This intransigence became especially evident in the conflicts over the majority principle in the Imperial diet during the Reformation, on the eve of the Thirty Years' War, and during the Prussian-Austrian dualism of the eighteenth century. The impracticality of enforcing central decisions over and against the opposition of the powerful Imperial members led to a constant pressure to reach consensual decisions in the main Imperial institutions, because anything else ran the risk of complete political paralysis. When the different parties could not reach a compromise, disputes and conflicts often dragged on for many decades.

11. The Empire's ability to adapt itself to changing circumstances was not uniform throughout the different phases of its history. The Imperial members responded to the structural challenges of the late Middle Ages by cooperating closely with one another and implementing an important set of institutional reforms. The Imperial institutions

survived the trials of the Reformation era and even became stronger in the process. Empire-wide cooperation and the liberties of the individual members were not mutually exclusive. It was only in the late sixteenth century, with the buildup of confessional camps, that consensual decisions became less frequent and the obstruction of many of the Empire's mechanisms more common. The end of the Thirty Years' War demonstrated once again that the Empire could endure as a political body only by striking the right balance between the liberties of its estates, the emperor's authority, and the continuing functioning of Imperial institutions. Only in the eighteenth century did it become evident that the Empire could not compete with the rising influence of its more powerful members. Having withstood Luther, Gustavus Adolphus, and Louis XIV, the Holy Roman Empire of the German Nation ultimately fell victim to its inability to reform itself.

THE ROMAN-GERMAN EMPERORS OF THE EARLY MODERN PERIOD

1493–1519	Maximilian I
1519–1558	Charles V
1558–1564	Ferdinand I (Roman king from 1531)
1564–1576	Maximilian II (Roman king from 1562)
1576–1612	Rudolf II (Roman king from 1575)
1612–1619	Matthias
1619–1637	Ferdinand II
1637–1657	Ferdinand III (Roman king from 1636)
1658–1705	Leopold I
1705–1711	Joseph I (Roman king from 1690)
1711–1740	Charles VI
1742–1745	Charles VII (Charles Albert of Bavaria)
1745–1765	Francis I (Francis Stephen of Lorraine)
1765–1790	Joseph II (Roman king from 1764)
1790–1792	Leopold II
1792–1806	Francis II

SELECT BIBLIOGRAPHY

SOURCEBOOKS

Arno Buschmann, ed. *Kaiser und Reich*, vol. 2 of 2 vols. 2nd ed. Baden-Baden, 1994.

Heinz Duchhardt, ed. *Quellen zur Verfassungsentwicklung des Heiligen Römischen Reiches deutscher Nation (1495–1806)*. Darmstadt, 1983.

Hanns Hubert Hofmann, ed. *Quellen zum Verfassungsorganismus des Heiligen Römischen Reiches deutscher Nation 1495–1815*. Darmstadt, 1976.

Rainer A. Müller, ed. *Deutsche Geschichte in Quellen und Darstellungen*, vol. 3, *Reformationszeit*; vol. 4, *Gegenreformation und Dreissigjähriger Krieg*; vol. 5, *Zeitalter des Absolutismus*; vol. 6: *Von der Französischen Revolution bis zum Wiener Kongress, 1789–1815*. Stuttgart, 1996–1997.

Samuel Pufendorf. *Die Verfassung des deutschen Reiches*, ed. Horst Denzer. Erstausgabe, 1667; Stuttgart, 1994.

Peter H. Wilson, ed. *The Thirty Years War: A Sourcebook*. Basingstoke, 2010.

GENERAL SURVEYS AND INTERPRETATIONS

Jason Philip Coy, Benjamin Marschke, and David Warren Sabean, eds. *The Holy Roman Empire, Reconsidered. Spektrum: Publications of the German Studies Association*, vol. 1. New York and Oxford, 2010.

Robert J. W. Evans, Michael Schaich, and Peter H. Wilson, eds. *The Holy Roman Empire 1495–1806. Studies of the German Historical Institute London*. Oxford, 2011.

Robert J. W. Evans and Peter H. Wilson, eds. *The Holy Roman Empire, 1495–1806: A European Perspective*. Leiden, 2011.

John Gagliardo. *Germany under the Old Regime 1600–1790*. London, 1991.

Axel Gotthard. *Das Alte Reich 1495–1806*, 3rd ed. Darmstadt, 2006.

Klaus Herbers and Helmut Neuhaus. *Das Heilige Römische Reich*. Cologne, 2010.

Beat Kümin. "Political Culture in the Holy Roman Empire." *German History* 27, no. 1 (2009): 131–144.

150 ◆ Select Bibliography

Wolfgang Reinhard, ed. *Gebhard Handbuch der deutschen Geschichte*, vols. 9–12; vol. 10, *Frühe Neuzeit bis zum Ende des Alten Reiches (1495–1806)*. Rev. ed. Stuttgart, 2001–2006.

Heinz Schilling, Werner Heun, and Jutta Götzmann, eds. *Altes Reich und neue Staaten 1495 bis 1806*, 2 vols. (exhibition catalog and essays). Dresden, 2006.

Georg Schmidt. *Geschichte des Alten Reiches: Staat und Nation in der Frühen Neuzeit 1495–1806*. München, 1999.

Robert Scribner and Sheila Ogilvie, eds. *Germany. A New Social and Economic History*, 2 vols. London, 1996.

Barbara Stollberg-Rilinger. *The Emperor's Old Clothes: Constitutional History and the Symbolic Language of the Holy Roman Empire*. New York and Oxford, 2015.

James Allan Vann, ed. *The Old Reich: Essays on German Political Institutions 1495–1806*. Brussels, 1974.

Joachim Whaley. *Germany and the Holy Roman Empire*, 2 vols. Oxford, 2011.

Dietmar Willoweit. *Deutsche Verfassungsgeschichte: Vom Frankenreich bis zur Wiedervereinigung Deutschlands*. 6th ed. Munich, 2009.

Peter H. Wilson. *The Holy Roman Empire: A Thousand Years of Europe's History*. London, 2016.

———. *The Holy Roman Empire 1495–1806*. 2nd ed. Basingstoke, 2011.

THE EMPIRE IN THE LATE MIDDLE AGES AND THE AGE OF "IMPERIAL REFORM"

Karl-Friedrich Krieger. *König, Reich und Reichsreform im Spätmittelalter*. Vol. 14 of *Enzyklopädie deutscher Geschichte*. Munich, 1992.

Peter Moraw. "Versuch über die Entstehung des Reichstags." In *Politische Ordnungen und soziale Kräfte im alten Reich*, ed. Hermann Weber. Wiesbaden, 1980, 1–36.

———. *Von offener Verfassung zu gestalteter Verdichtung: Das Reich im späten Mittelalter 1250–1490*. Berlin, 1985.

Ernst Schubert. *Einführung in die deutsche Geschichte im Spätmittelalter*. 2nd ed. Darmstadt, 1998.

Hermann Wiesflecker. *Kaiser Maximilian I: Das Reich, Österreich und Europa an der Wende zur Neuzeit*, 5 vols. Munich, 1971–1986.

THE AGE OF REFORMATION AND CONFESSIONALIZATION

Peter Blickle. *From the Communal Reformation to the Revolution of the Common Man*. Leiden, 1998.

Wim Blockmans. *Emperor Charles V, 1500–1558.* London, 2002.

Thomas A. Brady. *German Histories in the Age of Reformations, 1400–1650.* Cambridge, 2009.

———. *Turning Swiss: Cities and the Empire 1450–1550.* Cambridge, 1985.

C. Scott Dixon. *The Reformation in Germany.* Oxford, 2002.

Axel Gotthard. *Der Augsburger Religionsfrieden.* Münster, 2004.

Martin Heckel. *Deutschland im konfessionellen Zeitalter.* Göttingen, 1983.

Ronnie P. C. Hsia. *Social Discipline in the Reformation: Central Europe 1550–1750.* London, 1989.

Alfred Kohler. *Karl V, 1500–1558: Eine Biographie.* Munich, 1999.

Albrecht P. Luttenberger. "Reichspolitik und Reichstag unter Karl V. Formen zentralen politischen Handelns." In *Aus der Arbeit an den Reichstagen unter Kaiser Karl V,* ed. Heinrich Lutz and Alfred Kohler. Göttingen, 1986, 18–68.

Horst Rabe. *Deutsche Geschichte 1500–1600: Das Jahrhundert der Glaubensspaltung.* Munich, 1991.

Wolfgang Reinhard. "Gegenreformation als Modernisierung? Prolegomena einer Theorie des konfessionellen Zeitalters." *Archiv für Reformationsgeschichte* 68 (1977): 226–251.

Heinz Schilling. *Aufbruch und Krise: Deutschland 1517–1648: Das Reich und die Deutschen.* Berlin, 1998.

Anton Schindling and Walter Ziegler, eds. *Die Territorien des Reiches im Zeitalter der Reformation und Konfessionalisierung,* 7 vols. Münster, 1989–1997.

Robert W. Scribner and C. Scott Dixon. *The German Reformation.* 2nd ed. Basingstoke, 2003.

THE THIRTY YEARS' WAR AND THE PEACE OF WESTPHALIA

Johannes Arndt. *Der Dreissigjährige Krieg 1618–1648.* Stuttgart, 2009.

Ronald Asch. *The Thirty Years War: The Holy Roman Empire and Europe 1618–48.* London, 1997.

Johannes Burkhardt. *Der Dreissigjährige Krieg.* Neue Historische Bibliothek. Frankfurt/Main, 1992.

Klaus Bussmann and Heinz Schilling, eds. *1648. Krieg und Frieden in Europa* (exhibition catalog), 2 vols. Göttingen, 1998.

Derek Croxton. "The Peace of Westphalia of 1648 and the Origins of Sovereignty." *International History Review* 21 (1999): 569–591.

Fritz Dickmann. *Der Westfälische Frieden.* 6th ed. Münster, 1972.

Heinz Duchhardt, ed. *Der Westfälische Friede: Diplomatie—politische Zäsur—kulturelles Umfeld—Rezeptionsgeschichte.* Munich, 1998.

Christoph Kampmann. *Europa und das Reich im Dreissigjährigen Krieg.* Stuttgart, 2008.

Paul Münch. *Das Jahrhundert des Zwiespalts: Deutschland 1600–1700.* Stuttgart, Berlin, and Cologne, 1999.

Volker Press. *Kriege und Krisen: Deutschland 1600–1715.* Munich, 1991.

Konrad Repgen. *Dreissigjähriger Krieg und Westfälischer Friede: Studien und Quellen.* Rechts- und staatswissenschaftliche Veröffentlichungen der Görres-Gesellschaft, vol. 81. Paderborn, 1981.

Peter H. Wilson. "New Perspectives on the Thirty Years War." *German History* 23, no. 2 (2005): 237–261.

———. *The Thirty Years War: Europe's Tragedy.* Cambridge, 2009.

FROM THE PEACE OF WESTPHALIA TO THE END OF THE EMPIRE

Karl Otmar Freiherr von Aretin. *Das Alte Reich 1648–1806*, 3 vols. Stuttgart, 1993–1997.

———. *Vom Deutschen Reich zum Deutschen Bund.* Göttingen, 1980.

Ronald G. Asch. "Estates and Princes after 1648: The Consequences of the Thirty Years War." *German History* 6 (1988): 113–132.

Timothy C. W. Blanning, *The French Revolution in Germany: Occupation and Resistance in the Rhineland 1792–1892.* Oxford, 1983.

Wolfgang Burgdorf. *Ein Weltbild verliert seine Welt: Der Untergang des Alten Reiches und die Generation von 1806.* 2nd ed. Munich, 2009.

Heinz Duchhardt. *Altes Reich und europäische Staatenwelt 1648–1806.* Vol. 4 of *Enzyklopädie deutscher Geschichte.* Munich, 1990.

Johann Wolfgang von Goethe. *From My Life: Poetry and Truth*, vol. 1. New York, 1987.

Hans Gross. *Empire and Sovereignty: A History of the Public Law Literature in the Holy Roman Empire 1599–1804.* Chicago, 1973.

Karl Härter. *Reichstag und Revolution 1789–1806.* Göttingen, 1992.

Gabriele Haug-Moritz. "Kaisertum und Parität: Reichspolitik und Konfessionen nach dem Westfälischen Frieden." *Zeitschrift für Historische Forschung* 19 (1992): 445–482.

Michael Hochedlinger. *Austria's Wars of Emergence 1683–1797.* Harlow, 2003.

Charles W. Ingrao, ed. *Imperial Principalities on the Eve of Revolution: The Lay Electorates. German History* 20, no. 3 (special issue). London, 2002.

Helmut Neuhaus. "Das Ende des Alten Reiches." In *Das Ende von Grossreichen*, ed. Helmut Altrichter and Helmut Neuhaus. Erlangen, 1996, 185–209.

Volker Press. "Die kaiserliche Stellung im Reich zwischen 1648 und 1740—

Versuch einer Neubewertung." In *Das Alte Reich: Ausgewählte Aufsätze*, ed. Johannes Kunisch, Berlin, 1997, 189–222.

Heinz Schilling. *Höfe und Allianzen: Deutschland 1648–1763.* Berlin, 1989.

Mack Walker. *Johann Jakob Moser and the Holy Roman Empire of the German Nation.* Chapel Hill, 1989.

Peter H. Wilson. *German Armies: War and German Politics 1648–1806.* London, 1998.

PARTICULAR INSTITUTIONS

Rosemarie Aulinger. *Das Bild des Reichstags im 16. Jahrhundert: Beiträge zu einer typologischen Analyse schriftlicher und bildlicher Quellen.* Göttingen, 1980.

Bernhard Diestelkamp. *Recht und Gericht im Heiligen Römischen Reich.* Frankfurt/Main, 1999.

———, ed. *Das Reichskammergericht in der deutschen Geschichte.* Cologne, Weimar, and Wien, 1990.

Jeroen Duindam. *Vienna and Versailles: The Courts of Europe's Dynastic Rivals, 1550–1780.* Cambridge, 2003.

Stefan Ehrenpreis, Andreas Gotzmann, and Stephan Wendehorst. "Probing the Legal History of the Jews in the Holy Roman Empire—Norms and Their Application." *Jahrbuch des Simon-Dubnow-Instituts* 2 (2003): 409–487.

Marc R. Forster. *Catholic Revival in the Age of Baroque: Religious Identity in Southwest Germany, 1550–1750.* Cambridge, 2001.

Susanne Friedrich. *Drehscheibe Regensburg: Das Informations- und Kommunikationssystem des Immerwährenden Reichstags um 1700.* Berlin, 2007.

Ralf Peter Fuchs. "The Supreme Court of the Holy Roman Empire." *Sixteenth-Century Journal* 34 (2001): 9–21.

Andreas Gotzmann and Stephan Wendehorst, eds. *Juden im Recht: Neue Zugänge zur Rechtsgeschichte der Juden im Alten Reich. Zeitschrift für Historische Forschung* 39. Berlin, 2007.

Peter Claus Hartmann, ed. *Reichskirche—Mainzer Kurstaat—Reichskanzler.* Frankfurt/Main, 2001.

Gerhard Köbler. *Historisches Lexikon der deutschen Länder: Die deutschen Territorien vom Mittelalter bis zur Gegenwart.* 4th ed. Munich, 1992.

Peter Moraw. "Hoftag und Reichstag von den Anfängen im Mittelalter bis 1806." In *Parlamentsrecht und Parlamentspraxis in der Bundesrepublik Deutschland: Ein Handbuch*, ed. Hans-Peter Schneider and Wolfgang Zeh. Berlin and New York, 1989, 3–47.

Rita Sailer. *Untertanenprozesse vor dem Reichskammergericht: Rechtsschutz gegen die Obrigkeit in der zweiten Hälfte des 18. Jahrhunderts.* Cologne, Weimar, and Wien, 1999.

Ingrid Scheurmann, ed. *Frieden durch Recht: Das Reichskammergericht von 1495 bis 1806* (exhibition catalog). Mainz, 1994.

Anton Schindling. *Die Anfänge des Immerwährenden Reichstags zu Regensburg: Ständevertretung und Staatskunst nach dem Westfälischen Frieden.* Mainz, 1991.

Anton Schindling and Walter Ziegler, eds. *Die Kaiser der Neuzeit 1519– 1918: Heiliges Römisches Reich, Österreich, Deutschland.* Munich, 1990.

Klaus Schlaich. "Maioritas—protestatio—itio in partes—corpus Evangelicorum: Das Verfahren im Reichstag des Heiligen Römischen Reiches deutscher Nation nach der Reformation." *Zeitschrift der Savigny-Stiftung für Rechtsgeschichte Kanonistische Abteilung* 94 (1977): 264–299; 95 (1978): 139–179.

Winfried Schulze. "Peasant Resistance in Sixteenth- and Seventeenth-Century Germany in a European Context." In *Religion, Politics, and Social Protest*, ed. Kaspar von Greyerz. London, 1984, 61–98.

———. *Reichskammergericht und Reichsfinanzverfassung im 16. und 17. Jahrhundert.* Wetzlar, 1989.

Barbara Stollberg-Rilinger. "Zeremoniell als politisches Verfahren: Rangordnung und Rangstreit als Strukturmerkmale des frühneuzeitlichen Reichstags." *Zeitschrift für Historische Forschung* 19 (1997): 91–132.

Michael Stolleis. *Geschichte des öffentlichen Rechts in Deutschland*, vol. 1, *Reichspublizistik und Policeywissenschaft 1600–1800.* Munich, 1988.

Mack Walker. *German Home Towns: Community, State, and General Estate, 1648–1871.* 2nd ed. Ithaca, 1998.

Bernd Herbert Wanger. *Kaiserwahl und Krönung im Frankfurt des 17. Jahrhunderts.* Frankfurt/Main, 1994.

Roger Wines. "The Imperial Circles: Princely Diplomacy and Imperial Reform 1681–1714." *Journal of Modern History* 39 (1967): 1–29.

Wolfgang Wüst, ed. *Reichskreis und Territorium: Die Herrschaft über der Herrschaft? Supraterritoriale Tendenzen in Politik, Kultur, Wirtschaft und Gesellschaft: Ein Vergleich süddeutscher Reichskreise.* Stuttgart, 2000.

THE IMAGE OF THE OLD REICH IN THE EYES OF CONTEMPORARIES AND IN MODERN HISTORIOGRAPHY

John Gagliardo. *Reich and Nation: The Holy Roman Empire as Idea and Reality 1763–1806.* Bloomington, 1980.

Rainer A. Müller, ed. *Bilder des Reiches.* Sigmaringen, 1997.

Jean Paul. *Siebenkäs*, ed. Klaus Pauler. München, 1991.

Wolfgang Reinhard. "Frühmoderner Staat und deutsches Monstrum: Die Entstehung des modernen Staates und das Alte Reich." *Zeitschrift für historische Forschung* 29 (2002): 339–358.

Heinz Schilling. "Reichs-Staat und frühneuzeitliche Nation der Deutschen oder teilmodernisiertes Reichssystem: Überlegungen zu Charakter und Aktualität des Alten Reiches." *Historische Zeitschrift* 272 (2001): 377–395.

Anton Schindling. "Kaiser, Reich und Reichsverfassung 1648–1806: Das neue Bild vom Alten Reich." In *Altes Reich, Frankreich und Europa: Politische, philosophische, und historische Aspekte des französischen Deutschlandbildes im 17. und 18. Jahrhundert*, ed. Olaf Asbach et al. Berlin, 2001, 25–54.

Georg Schmidt. "Das frühneuzeitliche Reich—komplementärer Staat und föderative Nation." *Historische Zeitschrift* 272 (2001): 371–400.

Matthias Schnettger, ed. *Imperium Romanum—irregulare corpus—Teutscher Reichs-Staat: Das Alte Reich im Verständnis der Zeitgenossen und der Historiographie*. Mainz, 2002.

Peter H. Wilson. "Still a Monstrosity? Some Reflections on Early Modern Statehood." *Historical Journal* 49 (2006): 565–576.

INDEX

Italicized page numbers indicate illustrations.